Studies and surveys
in comparative education

Titles in this series

Wastage in education : a world problem
A statistical study of wastage at school
Initiatives in education : a world profile for 1971-72
Constructive education for children
World problems in education : a brief analytical survey

World problems in education

A brief analytical survey

by Jean Thomas

A study prepared for the
International Bureau of
Education

The Unesco Press   Paris   1975

Published by
The Unesco Press
7, place de Fontenoy, 75700 Paris

Printed by Imprimerie Courvoisier
La Chaux-de-Fonds, Switzerland

ISBN 92-3-101297-5
French ed.: 92-3-201297-9

Preface

Although it is too early to talk of a tradition, the International Bureau of Education has, since it became part of Unesco in 1969, endeavoured to publish studies resulting from the work of the International Conference on Education in its series *Studies and surveys in comparative education*. The aim of this series is not to report on the discussions of the Conference but rather to offer to the general public, and especially to persons concerned with education, an integrated picture of a major problem such as the special theme to which part of the proceedings of each session of the Conference is devoted, or a more general study of major trends in education over a given period.

In 1973, the special theme at the thirty-fourth session of the International Conference on Education, was 'The relationship between education, training and employment with particular reference to secondary education', major trends in education being discussed in Plenary. Both subjects are dealt with in this work by Mr. Jean Thomas who, however, has probed more deeply in his study of the major problems faced by the Member States of Unesco. As he himself explains, he has taken as a basis the proceedings of international and national conferences organized by Unesco or by other organizations in the past two or three years, and the conclusions of certain more specialized meetings. The result is a wide-ranging survey of the most topical problems of education, presented in a logical sequence.

First, there is the education system as a whole, or rather the partial and comprehensive reforms which are emerging in all regions of the world, since education is expected to effect the profound changes taking place in society and find solutions to the most pressing problems. Then, a few delicate areas—secondary education, particularly with regard to the employment opportunities to which it provides access, higher education and the new horizons it opens up, and adult education, an unlimited and infinitely varied field. It may be recalled that these three topics have been discussed at large international conferences convened by Unesco : namely, at the thirty-fourth session of the International Conference on Education (Geneva, 1973), the second Conference of Ministers of Education of European Member States (Bucharest, 1973) and the third International Conference on Adult Education (Tokyo, 1972).

The publication in 1972, under the title *Learning to be*, of the report of the International Commission on the Development of Education, presided over by Mr. Edgar Faure, was an important milestone in the activities and thinking of Unesco. Its repercussions were by no means limited to the Organization, for the ideas it contains have been discussed in Member States and the reactions it generated gave rise to an animated discussion in Geneva in 1973. It is scarcely surprising, therefore, to find that this book devotes three chapters to the report. Two aspects of the latter seem to have made a particular impression on the author, who has accordingly seen fit to examine the part played by innovation in the search for new solutions to the problems of education, and the period of crisis apparently being experienced by international co-operation in educational matters.

In outlining this picture of the situation, the International Bureau of Education has been privileged in receiving the particularly enlightened assistance of Mr. Jean Thomas, Chairman of the French National Commission for Unesco. In order to accomplish his appointed task, he has drawn on his rich store of experience, acquired initially at Unesco when he held the post of Deputy Director-General, and later in the French Ministry of Education as Inspector-General of Public Education. He has also drawn on his personal conclusions on recent developments in education, which he has always observed with an attentive and critical eye. Credit is therefore due him for the originality of this study, in which the opinions he expresses are not necessarily those of Unesco.

The International Bureau of Education has another very special reason for appreciating this assistance. Mr. Jean Thomas has, in fact, been associated with the IBE for a very long time : he has many times headed the French Delegation to the International Conference on Education and, above all, he gave the Bureau a firm and well-informed leadership in his capacity as Chairman of the IBE Council for the first four years following its integration into Unesco. The Secretariat of the IBE therefore takes this opportunity to express, once again, its profound gratitude to Mr. Jean Thomas ; this study is only the most recent demonstration of a long and loyal collaboration.

Contents

Foreword

The objective I set myself in embarking on this necessarily brief study was to call attention to the major questions raised by education in the various countries of the world during a specific period, and to identify the main trends reflected by recent reforms. It may seem an ambitious goal. I cannot pretend to have been exhaustive or even to have picked out the main essentials ; in this field, some choices are always arbitrary. I took as my initial basis the topics proposed at international meetings dealing with problems of education. In 1972, in addition to the seventeenth session of the General Conference, Unesco convened its third International Conference on Adult Education. Going a little further back in time, I made use of the work of two regional conferences, that of Ministers of Education and Ministers responsible for Economic Planning in Latin America and the Caribbean and that of Ministers of Education and those responsible for Economic Planning in Asia, both of which were held in the second half of 1971. In 1973, the International Conference on Education held its thirty-fourth session ; later in the same year, the second Conference of Ministers of Education of European Member States was held.

These conferences are extremely useful in that they provide a focal point for the lengthy preparatory work involved, since each participating State is requested to submit a detailed report, along the lines of a pattern laid down by a questionnaire. These national reports which I have been able to consult have, by their diversity, proved to be an unparalleled source of information and ideas. The days are gone when governments used to make much of their achievements in the field of education ; nowadays they tend rather to dwell on their difficulties and problems. National reports and the statistics compiled in connexion with their preparation, preliminary studies by international secretariats, summary records of discussions and final resolutions—all provided me with a rich and varied source of information.

I also used the proceedings of small meetings, such as symposia, seminars and expert committees, convened during the same period in various regions of the world, either on the initiative of Unesco or under the auspices of other international agencies like the Organization for Economic Co-operation and Development (OECD) or certain regional or national bodies. The year 1972 was distinguished by an event of world-wide importance : the publication of the report of the International Commission on the Development of Education, called the Edgar Faure Commission after its president. The ideas expressed in the report provided the inspiration for the last three chapters of my study, as did the work to which it gave rise in a great many countries and in Unesco itself.

Yet apart from these relatively official publications, I felt it necessary to refer to a great many studies, published in various places, on the topics I had chosen. In this way it was possible to compare the views of governments with those of independent experts, whose opinions were strictly their own. Although I have tried to be as objective as possible in dealing with the information collected, I have made no attempt to refrain from asking questions in my turn, nor have I hesitated on occasion to express personal opinions or to draw on my own long experience. How can one talk about education without becoming involved in serious thought, discussion or even doubt ?

The task would have been beyond my powers had I not been able to rely on the support of a team of specialists renowned for their competence. I cannot over-emphasize my gratitude to Mr. Leo Fernig and his colleagues in the IBE. Without their advice, the documentation which they keep up to date, and the work of the Unesco Office of Statistics, I should never have succeeded (in so far as I have succeeded) in carrying out my appointed task.

I hope that this work, whose shortcomings I make no attempt to hide, may at least provide its readers with food for thought and perhaps throw some light on one of the most serious problems of our time.

J. Th.
October 1974

Chapter one

Education
on the move

In response to a questionnaire sent out by the International Bureau of Education on the principal changes which had occurred in 1972 and 1973, reports were submitted to the International Conference on Education by more than fifty States. On reading these reports and listening to the statements of many other delegations, an attentive reader's first impression is that, in all regions of the world, many profound changes are taking place in national systems of education. Comprehensive or partial reforms are being carried out in all countries without exception. Education is everywhere on the move.

The second impression gained from this impressive documentation is that the need for change is everywhere making itself felt. Whether in the young States of Africa or Asia, seeking an education system adapted to their needs and to their distinctive culture, or in countries with old-established schools and universities, the authorities—governments, parliaments, political parties—as well as advisory bodies and experts, are everywhere planning, adopting or carrying out new reforms. Change is rarely imposed by force ; it is desired, encouraged and brought about. Round about 1968, when Philip H. Coomb's book was published announcing 'The world educational crisis', the mere word crisis resounded like a terrible warning. In 1973, it is no longer appropriate to talk of a crisis in the sense of a sudden and temporary state of affairs. Change has become an accepted feature of education and a necessary condition for progress. Hence the new tone to be detected in official reports, in which expressions of satisfaction are encountered far less frequently than admissions that something is lacking.

Far from being embarrassed at drawing attention to their shortcomings or difficulties, educational authorities no longer shrink
from self-criticism, and one is much more inclined to believe
in them.

THE DIVERSITY OF REFORMS

Some of the reforms announced for 1973 stem from changes in a
country's general policy, brought about either by the advent of a
new régime, or by a particular party's rise to power.   In the
Argentine Republic, for example, the national Government formed
in May 1973 proclaimed the need for a new educational structure
based on the twin principles of nationalization and socialization.
In Dahomey, at the end of 1972, the Military Government set
education the objectives of upgrading national languages and
cultures and giving a new African slant to university courses.   On
the death of President Tubman, the new Head of State of Liberia
gave high priority to education, placing it immediately after agriculture and before health and communications.   In New Zealand,
the Labour Party, which came to power in November 1972,
hastened to announce a change of direction in education, the
details of which are to be decided upon at a national conference.
A new educational policy was also proclaimed in Pakistan, with
various objectives ranging from the preservation of Islamic values
to the importance to be attached to science and technology.

   In many other countries, the changes which occurred in 1973
are described as stages in the implementation of a reform adopted
earlier.   This is the case in Bulgaria, in particular, which
announces measures designed to ensure the gradual transition from
the old eleven-year type of education to the new ten-year system,
crowned by the establishment of comprehensive secondary schools.
Or in Spain, where a long series of decrees, orders and regulations
are being used to implement, with an equal blend of caution and
determination, the far-reaching general law on education promulgated in August 1970.   France has embarked on a reform of secondary education which has had a stormy passage and has not yet
assumed its final form.   Norway, while refraining from using the
magic words 'lifelong education', is nevertheless engaged in building up an integrated system from nursery school to adult education.

The United Kingdom, or rather England and Wales, has decided to raise the legal school-leaving age to 16. The new measures adopted by the Soviet Union also constitute a stage in the implementation of the guidelines laid down for the ninth Five-Year Plan by the twenty-fourth Communist Party Congress, held in the spring of 1971. And in this connexion it is noteworthy—because unusual— that a new regulation was adopted and has been brought into force by the Union Minister of Education setting out the rights of students: diligence, good behaviour, participation in social and sports activities and respect for national property. For most countries in this category, following Sweden's example, education seems to have been deliberately fitted into a context of continuous reform —that is to say once general principles and objectives have been established, reform proceeds as a succession of partial changes, which are themselves subject to later adjustments.

Two other States, very far apart in their level of economic development, are noteworthy for the boldness of their reforms. The authorities of Ethiopia, with the assistance of international organizations and of Unesco in particular, carried out a critical review of the entire education system and took stock of the efforts that had been made and of existing weaknesses and short-comings. They reached the alarming conclusion that, at the present rate, and even if major sacrifices were made, it would be impossible to provide schooling for the majority of the population before the middle of the next century. It was also a fact that a great many qualified individuals were unable to find employment and, beyond the confines of school, a vast number of adults would never become literate. In this disastrous situation, reforms were not enough ; a radical change of policy was called for and a totally different strategy had to be adopted. Although we shall revert to the thorny problem of educational strategies further on in this study, a tribute should be paid at this point to the courage with which the Ethiopian authorities decided on a change of course, and which at the same time led them to give priority to primary education and adult education, to plan new structures, new types of training and a new distribution of resources, and to try out hitherto neglected educational methods.

Japan, for its part, readily recognizes the historical significance of the decision taken by the Government, after having examined

the report of the Central Council for Education, to embark upon
a third general reform of the education system ; the first dates back
to the Meiji era in the early days of modern Japan, and the second
had taken place immediately after the last World War. Of all
the countries which submitted national reports on the years
1971-1972, Japan alone announced that its reform is part and parcel
of the lifelong education process, from the pre-primary stage up to
adult education ; it is also the only one to redefine the specific role
which school and university are called upon to play in this general
context. Indeed, there is no denying the fact that, so far, the hand-
ful of countries which have adopted the principle of lifelong education have been reluctant to accept its implications for that part
of education which is directed at young people in schools and
universities. Too often, lifelong education is confused with adult
education, or alternatively with continuous training. Japan has
thus taken a courageous stand, and it will be most interesting to see
how its experiment unfolds, since in the years to come it is very
likely to set an example for other countries.

METHODOLOGY OF REFORMS

It is equally enlightening to examine the various methods used
in planning reforms. As we have already seen, certain reforms
were brought about by political circumstances, as in the case of
Argentina, Dahomey, Liberia or Pakistan ; others, in the socialist
countries and particularly in Cuba, were the outcome of a political
decision, namely, guidelines laid down by the supreme bodies of
a party for the development of a specific plan. Education was
naturally included among these general guidelines.

   But in a good many other countries with different régimes, the
stages of reform follow the slow pace set by the work of experts,
partial experiments and consultations at various levels before any
decisions are reached. In Japan, for example, the subject was
discussed by several councils and committees, experiments were
conducted in a number of specially selected primary of secondary
schools, systematic research was done by specialized institutes, pilot
experiments were organized by radio and television companies
and several universities were associated with the project ; and this
entire lengthy process was considered necessary to the gradual

implementation of the reform, under the co-ordinating authority of a permanent deputy minister of education. In Japan, as elsewhere, educational reform is undoubtedly a political matter, since it affects the future of the nation ; however, the actual components of reform, like the bodies responsible for their development and co-ordination, have one feature in common, namely, a technical understanding of the needs of education.

In New Zealand, the idea of reform seems to have originated at a meeting of a group representing the various interests concerned, held in August 1971 in order to make an appraisal of the structures and curricula of the educational establishment. A booklet summarizing the ideas expressed during this meeting was widely circulated in the country and served as a basis for further reflexion. The views and criticism to which this booklet gave rise, and the conclusions of discussion groups consisting of educators, parents or ordinary citizens provided the basis for a national conference held in September 1972. This generated a great many suggestions, which in turn gave rise to decisions concerning reform. It is also interesting to note that the Labour Party, which came to power in November of that year, did not feel satisfied with the suggestions made and decided to organize another conference on the development of education in 1974, which it no doubt expects to produce a bolder plan of action. However this may be, the reform has provided an opportunity for democratic consultation on a major scale.

In Mexico, a broad assessment survey (or rather a 'sounding', to use a term closer in meaning to the original Spanish) of the problems of education was conducted throughout the country in 1971 at conferences or seminars, some regional and others national, with the participation of teachers, parents, pupils, industrialists or technicians, and all the results of this consultation were eventually processed by the Ministry of Education, which was responsible for working out the principles of reform.

The draft reform of secondary education, which is at present the main concern of the Ministry of Education in France, gave rise to a large-scale national symposium, in November 1973, which was prepared and organized under the auspices of a committee of eleven independent and eminent persons drawn from all walks of life. As might have been expected, the symposium failed to

reach agreement on certain essential matters on which views
differed, although it did arrive at unanimous conclusions on the
development of nursery schools, the strengthening of school medical services, the increased importance of remedial instruction, a
gradual reduction in the number of pupils in classes of over twenty-
five, the provision of more audio-visual facilities, an increase in
the school supplies and of transport facilities made available free
of charge at various educational levels from nursery school
upwards, and a reduction of differences in the training, salaries
and hours of work of school-teachers. Although the areas of agreement may seem small compared with those of disagreement (such
as the retention or abolition of various options in the lower secondary course, the effectiveness of streaming, or the future of the
baccalaureat), the national symposium nevertheless marked an
important new departure and a new style of consultation prior to
the finalization of a project for reform.

The United Kingdom has never inclined very much towards
planning. For this reason, the government White Paper of December 1972, entitled 'Education : a framework for expansion', is to be
welcomed as an important event, in that it outlines a ten-year plan
for education in England and Wales and proposes five major axes
of development : more schools for children under the age of five,
an extensive school-building programme, a teacher-recruitment
programme, new measures to improve the initial and further
training of teachers, and a new type of higher education and
corresponding qualification. Most of these measures had admittedly been suggested by committees or commissions, but it is nonetheless remarkable that, in a field in which local authorities play
a leading part, the British Government has, once more, initiated
major changes as a part of a relatively long-term plan.

The example of the United Kingdom leads us to consider two
apparently conflicting tendencies which emerge from this profusion
of reforms. The first is a tendency towards decentralization of the
structures of national education. In several countries, such as
Mexico and Pakistan, the Ministry of Education has delegated some
of its responsibilities to new administrative levels which are in
closer contact with everyday reality. Algeria, Iran and Italy
recently divided their territory into educational districts or regions
in the interest of administrative simplification and flexibility. Even

a highly centralized country like France had already gone a long way in this direction, not only by granting complete autonomy to its universities, but also by strengthening the powers and increasing the responsibilities of the regional education officers. Decentralization thus seems to answer the needs of a new type of education.

But in countries where education is already very largely decentralized, a reverse trend may be detected, for the federal authorities are beginning to take bolder initiatives. The reason for this is often of a financial nature. In the United States, for example, the share of educational expenditure borne by the Federal Government is steadily increasing. In 1972, of the $50,000 million spent each year to maintain State primary and secondary schools, only 7 per cent was provided by the Federal Government, 41 per cent being contributed by the States and 52 per cent by local authorities. Since local spending was for the most part financed by real estate taxes, serious inequalities arose reflecting differences in the value of land and the yield from taxes between one region and another. Indeed, some local authorities were obliged to resort to unfortunate expedients such as shortening the school day, dismissing staff and postponing the purchase of necessary equipment. This resulted in considerable discontent and posed a threat to the fundamental principle of equality of educational opportunity. Private schools and even famous universities were still more seriously affected by the crisis, finding themselves obliged to increase their fees, at the risk of jeopardizing the recruitment of students. A presidential commission was therefore instructed to carry out a nation-wide survey on the financing of education, and its findings prompted Congress to adopt new legislation. Although there may have been no change in the principle of the sovereignty of individual states in educational matters, the federal authorities will now be in a position to give more active support to educational establishments for the benefit of the least privileged communities and ethnic groups. Thus, by means of subsidies, the United States Federal Government will be able to take more frequent and more effective action in a field which for a long time remained outside its direct control.

Similar problems and solutions are to be observed in Australia—another State with a federal structure. So far, in theory, only financial matters are being dealt with. But in the Federal

Republic of Germany, much more has been done. It is a known fact that, although the 1949 Constitution stipulates that all education shall be State-controlled, in practice it transfers this responsibility to the governments of the *Länder*. True, it is the task of the Standing Conference of Ministers of Education to ensure a measure of co-ordination, but its decisions, which have to be unanimous, never amount to more than recommendations to the *Länder*, which alone decide whether or not to implement them. In recent years, however, a generally recognized need has emerged for a reform of secondary education, whose highly complex structures are regarded as out of date, and of vocational education, which is now being questioned. A joint educational planning commission, in which representatives of the Federal Government participated on an equal footing with those of the *Länder*, had to be set up in order to decide upon the principles which were to constitute the basis of the reform. The reform of the commission, submitted in July 1972, recommends urgent measures with far-reaching implications, such as the extension of pre-primary education, the improvement of technical courses, the establishment of a new type of secondary school and a rapid increase in the number of university places. It will undoubtedly be the responsibility of the *Länder* to implement the reform, with full autonomy in their decision making. Yet it is clear that, where the national interest is at stake, the Federal Government does not hesitate to step in and play an increasingly active role.

Decentralization in highly centralized countries and strengthening of the central authority's powers in highly decentralized countries : these two tendencies, which are not so much contradictory as complementary, are certainly necessary conditions for progress in education. But they have never emerged so plainly as in the years 1972-1973.

THE PROBLEMS PERSIST

This burning desire for change and the proliferation of reforms are, according to the reports of many countries, the outward signs of an unease which is growing as time passes, since the same problems linger on. The hopes that these countries had placed in planning are often dashed, as Dahomey and Thailand, with admirable frankness, admit. A rapid analysis of those problems to which no solution has yet been found will make it easier to form a clearer idea of the actual situation in education during the past few years.

Educational wastage

This is perhaps the oldest and best-known problem, and has lost none of its gravity. In Latin America as much as in Africa and Asia, and in the Argentine Republic as well as in Nigeria and Thailand, a great many children continue to drop out of school in the early years of their education. Malaysia observes, with bitter irony, that whereas the demand for education is growing more pressing and requires heavier sacrifices from the nation, the number of school dropouts shows no signs of diminishing.

Educational retardation

Failures and grade repetition are always the scourge of primary education, and often that of secondary education, too. The developing countries are the most hard hit : in Dahomey, calculations show that only one pupil in five entering school reaches his fifth year ; in Zaire, 80 per cent of children at primary school do not get as far as the primary school-leaving certificate. But failures and repetition do not spare the more highly developed countries either : Belgium's report estimates them at 28 per cent for primary education as a whole ; in France, recent statistics bring this proportion up to nearly 50 per cent for the last two years of this educational level.

Factors resulting in inequality

The fact that the schooling provided in the towns is much more thorough than in rural areas is confirmed by the reports of Cuba, Ethiopia, Iraq, Jordan, Liberia, Malaysia, Mali, the Philippines and Romania. The report from Dahomey provides alarming details in that whereas the average school enrolment rate at the primary level is 30 per cent, it is 68 per cent in the capital but only 12 per cent in remote areas. Inequality appears in other ways, too, for Jordan courageously admits that there are far fewer girls at schools than boys. We saw in the United States that the poorest communities and ethnic minorities still do not have the same facilities and do not receive an education of the same quality as the rest of the population. Inequality of educational opportunity is thus felt everywhere to be one of the most serious and least tolerable problems, and one is forced to admit that, as the causes of inequality are more social than educational, the school is not in a position to apply the most effective solutions. The heaviest burden of responsibility lies with society. Even the socialist countries have not eliminated all factors contributing to inequality. The big cities offer more numerous and more varied resources than are to be found in rural areas, and the situation of ethnic or linguistic minorities as well as differences in the cultural level of families, are still obstacles to equality of opportunity. The relationship between the education system and social structures now lies at the heart of most educational problems. This relationship does not, in any case, operate in one direction only because, although school to a large extent reflects the state of society, it is also a powerful element in social change. We shall see the impact of this dialectical tension on each of the major questions which will be tackled in this study. Nevertheless, whatever the recognized or suspected causes of inequality of opportunity, all education systems are now trying to eliminate them so far as their resources permit.

The search for a remedy

No one has yet found a completely effective solution to the problem of school dropouts. Whether in developing countries, like India, or in the deprived areas of industrialized countries, like southern Italy, most families who take their children away from school are driven by the need to make their children work and contribute in one way or another to the upkeep of their family. The authorities can best take action against this tendency through campaigns of information or persuasion rather than through coercion. This means that progress in this respect is very slow.

     Recent experiments in education, on the other hand, provide remedies for retardation at school such as automatic passage from one class to the next at the end of the year, the abolition of qualifying exams for the next class, streaming, the organization of remedial classes and the replacement of periodic examinations by continuous assessment. The reports submitted by various countries, and particularly Belgium, France, Italy, New Zealand and Spain, reveal that such solutions are finding increasing favour ; but these are almost all developed countries. Nevertheless, among the developing countries, the Philippines has announced the introduction of a system of continuous progression which enables each child to transfer from one class to another at his own pace. At the beginning of each school year, the teachers decide what standard each of their pupils has attained so that they can be taught at the level they have reached. Yet, it must be admitted that these methods are not accepted by all teachers. At the national symposium held in France in 1973 to consider the draft reform of secondary education, it was found that although there was unanimity in favour of remedial education, this was not true of streaming, some of the most influential trade union organizations objecting that this system accentuated selection, and even segregation, among children at school. This tends to prove that there is no such thing as final and universally accepted progress in education.

Two of the possible ways of eliminating inequality of opportunity resulting from differences in the social and cultural background of schoolchildren were specifically mentioned in recommendations adopted by previous sessions of the International Conference on Education. The first consists of freely organized activities in school but distinct from school work, and the second is pre-primary education. Activities of the first kind are regarded favourably in many of the most developed countries, and take such forms as social and cultural centres in schools, clubs, artistic or dramatic activities, and educational games to stimulate the creative faculties. It must nevertheless be admitted that these solutions are frequently expensive and call both for equipment and specially trained teachers or leaders. These are all things which the most underprivileged countries rightly consider to be a luxury they cannot afford.

The other solution is to develop pre-primary education. Very many of the national reports submitted to the last session of the International Conference on Education indicated that this solution is attracting an increasing number of countries—Western European, the socialist States, or even developing countries like the Libyan Arab Republic and Senegal. The statement by the British Government revealed a ten-year plan to establish a large number of schools for children under five. In New Zealand, the Department of Education has just decided, on the basis of a report by a specially appointed committee of inquiry, to provide considerable financial aid to encourage the rapid development of nursery schools in each district. This attitude seems to mark a turning point in the thinking of the English-speaking countries where public opinion, whilst admitting the advantages of such schools, has so far hesitated to entrust the school with responsibilities which should belong, first and foremost, to the family. The joint committee set up in the Federal Republic of Germany by the Federal authorities and those of the *Länder* also recommended that the number of schools and available places in the pre-primary sector as a whole should be rapidly increased. Spain, for its part, is turning towards a system of pre-school education divided into two successive levels, namely, the kindergarten for children from two to three years of age, and the nursery school for children from four to five. Since many other countries like Bulgaria, Finland, France, Greece, Hungary, Norway, Poland and the Soviet Union mention spectacular progress with this kind of education, the inescapable conclusion is that pre-school education seems to be the solution of the future.

Here too, however, reservations must be expressed. In the most underprivileged countries, where it is proving so difficult to make primary education widely available, any extra burden is a luxury which cannot yet be contemplated. Secondly, there are very few countries where pre-primary education is part of the education system ; it is essentially voluntary in nature and almost everywhere it is for the family to choose. Finally, and most important, it is still ambiguous in character. Among the reasons put forward by governments in its favour, the desire to help mothers obliged to work away from home is accompanied by arguments of an educational, psychological or social nature. In other words, nursery schools, and very rightly too, continue to play the role of crêches. The most farsighted advocates of kindergartens and nursery schools nevertheless assign them a different and more ambitious purpose, for in these schools, particularly if they are maintained by public funds, children of all social classes mix together and learn to share the same games and exercises. At an age which psychologists agree is decisive in the shaping of the personality and the learning of mental processes, pre-primary education is a powerful force for democratization, a preparation for future school work and an effective remedy for inequalities in the social and cultural environment.

There is yet one more point on which views differ, for it is claimed by some—and they are in the majority—that nursery schools do not provide instruction to children at that age but offer a form of character training, while others feel that the nursery school is tending to become the first stage of primary education. This would seem to be true of the Netherlands where preparations are being made, as part of a general plan, to introduce primary education for children from four to twelve years of age. Obviously then, the success of pre-school education and a certain confusion of ideas about its advantages and aims are not mutually exclusive.

Ways of remedying the other causes of inequality are well known. There is no shortage of solutions, which may take the form of providing country children with the same educational facilities as town children, providing the same facilities for girls and boys, or ensuring that the facilities available to all minorities and underprivileged communities are of the same standard as those available to the rest of the population. Among the developing countries, such as Algeria, Cuba, Dahomey, Ethiopia, Iraq, Jordan, Liberia, Malaysia, Mali and the Philippines, to say nothing of those as industrialized as Romania, very few indeed have failed to include in their plans relatively bold projects for the development of education in rural areas. What most of these countries lack is not imagination or will but money.

There is a final, and possibly the cruellest, factor which breeds inequality, namely, the handicaps suffered by children as a result of physical or mental disorders or of accidents or incurable diseases. Are we to believe that, for obscure reasons, the number of such children is tending to increase, or can it be that society has become aware of its responsibilities towards them? The fact remains that the education of handicapped children is mentioned more and more frequently in national reports, even in those from developing countries like the Libyan Arab Republic.

The inadaptability of education systems

Here we approach the biggest and most widespread problem of all and one which has, for some years, been the favourite theme of the reproaches levelled at modern education. However, as soon as the now commonplace arguments are left behind we are obliged to face up to the following question : by reference to what criteria can one assert that a given form of education is unsuitable ? The most obvious example is that of the former colonies which, on achieving independence, inherited the education system of the countries to which they had formerly belonged. The reports from Ghana, Jordan and Senegal contain detailed studies of this situation and of its effects which are felt even today. The point is so obvious as to need no labouring that an imported style of education, even if introduced with the best of intentions, can never correspond to the social structures, cultural traditions, economic needs or national aspirations of States which have become independent and assumed responsibility for their own identity. The situation becomes yet more complicated in countries which want to use one of their most widely spoken dialects as a language of instruction. In this case, as in Nigeria or Malaysia, all the problems involved have to be faced at the same time, i.e. preparatory language courses, the preparation of textbooks, the development of suitable methods, and teacher training, to say nothing of the danger of a lowering of standards in the knowledge of the language of communication which is still needed at the higher levels of education.

The poor results achieved by education, the abandonment of rural areas by young people leaving school, the danger of unemployment among new graduates, the crushing burden of expenditure imposed on their countries by existing education systems, and the criticism that such systems are basically unsuitable are so many factors generating bitterness on the part of African thinkers. Some state outright that 'the system of education in Africa must be re-invented'. Referring back to the precolonial era, they are quick to point out that although Africa did not have schools at that time, it was, nevertheless, not without education. This traditional and customary education taught children and young people 'through living and doing'. Every adult was, in some way or other, a 'teacher'. For his part, an educator from Niger states that 'leaving aside any nostalgia for the past, any romantic regrets and sentimental lamentation, traditional African education is a rich source of instruction and a subject for reflexion for anyone who wishes to give even a minimum amount of serious thought to the problems of education and instruction in the Black Africa of today. Unlike colonial education, which simply set itself down by the side of traditional African education, ignoring it and despising it in practice, any new concept of instruction and education which aspires to be valid and satisfy the present conditions and future prospects of Black Africa must, if it is to be genuinely national and popular in nature, borrow certain aspects of traditional education and integrate them into a modern, forward-looking educational system and, in addition, exist side by side with traditional education for a while and endeavour to influence it'. [1]

The Round Table held in Dakar in February 1972 by Unesco's Regional Office for Education in Africa, reached conclusions which, although possibly expressed in less ambitious terms, were based on the same ideas. There was a broad consensus on the inadequacy and unsuitability of present education systems and on the need for a different kind of education for young people. In the opinion of the experts from twelve African countries who attended the Round Table, present systems rested on axioms. Their coherence was based on a continuous and uninterrupted curriculum. 'The only point of entry into the system is at zero and you keep going until you leave. If you depart from the curriculum you return to it only in exceptional cases. A path has thus been laid out for you to follow .... You cannot enter secondary school until you have completed your primary education ; you cannot go to university without having passed through the previous stages.' In contrast to this system of linear progression, those attending the Round Table suggested other forms of education which were not incompatible, which were applicable to children or adults and did not require their removal from the context of everyday life and development activities.

Examples of this revival of customary education adapted to modern conditions, and of this amalgam of tradition with the requirements of development can perhaps be found in certain out-of-school educational experiments at present being conducted

1. These words by President Julius Nyerere, Mr. Abdou Moumouni and Mr. F. Agblemagnon were taken from the *Bulletin de liaison pédagogique de l'enseignement technique et de la formation professionnelle*, no. 15, June 1974, published by AUDECAM in Paris.

in various African countries ; they include the spontaneous forms
of education and preparation for collective work in Nigeria, young
farmers' clubs in Dahomey, rural polytechnic centres in Kenya,
cultural and community activities in Cameroon, as well as many
other experiments, particularly in Mali.

Although feeling about the unsuitability of education systems
is particularly strong in Africa, the vast majority of other countries,
whatever their level of development, also indicate that this factor
is the main reason for the reforms which have already been
adopted or which are planned. The normal functioning of education systems is no longer producing the results which the nation
is entitled to expect of them. School dropouts, the poor performance of education and inequality of opportunity are leading critical
observers and even the authorities to question some of the
principles on which these systems are based. Moreover, there is
a growing lack of correspondence between the skills of young
graduates, products of the education system, and the needs of the
economy. Most of the changes demanded in education, such as
the reform of structures, the reform of curricula and methods of
evaluation, a new type of relationship between teachers and pupils,
and educational innovations, are aimed at a better adaptation of
education to society's present circumstances and to forseeable
conditions.

Beneath this apparent unanimity, one can nevertheless discern
different and even opposing trends. Although the principle of
selection on the basis of merit through examinations and tests
reflected a basic democratic goal at the time of the French Revolution, and although it still constitutes the cornerstone of the education systems of most socialist States, it now stands condemned,
precisely in the name of democratization, by a large segment of
public opinion in Western countries. Attitudes in this respect
cannot be unanimous since they are based far more on ideologies,
political opinions and prejudices than on objective judgements.
This explains why the solutions adopted or recommended are so
varied.

The only entirely objective criterion possible is the degree of
adaptation to the needs of the economy. The example of rigorous
educational planning in the light of anticipated economic requirements comes from the Soviet Union. The European people's

democracies were the first to be convinced by the results obtained of the merits of planning, and the same, although more flexible, course was then followed by many Western countries with liberal systems of government. The influence of international organizations, particularly Unesco, subsequently led to its adoption by developing countries, as planning was represented to them as being essential for development. However, some of these countries are now showing signs of disenchantment ; the plans drawn up almost fifteen years ago in Addis Ababa by African Ministers of Education proved to be impractical, despite efforts by the States concerned and international assistance. A primary school enrolment rate of 71 per cent in 1970 and of 100 per cent in 1980 was selected as the target for Africa as a whole ; however, in 1972 the rate did not exceed 49 per cent. Nor can the school enrolment effort be maintained at the planned rate outside Africa, and Thailand, for example, admits that, owing to rapid population growth, it is unable to educate all its children. Although the Ministers of Education of Latin America at their most recent meeting, held in Venezuela in December 1972, took note of the progress which had been achieved, they also expressed concern at certain serious shortcomings ; indeed, according to their estimate more than 8 million children between seven and twelve years of age had not yet received any education in this region of the world. (Table 1 gives an idea of the growth in the school enrolment rate throughout the world during the decade from 1960 to 1970.)

Passing from quantitative to qualitative considerations, it must be admitted that the results obtained in many Third World countries are hardly more satisfactory. Dahomey, Egypt, Syria, and Thailand refer to the mediocre quality of their education, whether at primary or at secondary level, and to the inadequate qualifications of their teachers. The blunt candour of the report from Zaire sounds an even more alarming note in stating that the educational level is as low in secondary schools as in primary schools ; two-thirds of the 65,000 primary school-teachers employed are officially recognized as not having the necessary training. For many countries the shortage and inadequacy of teachers remain a matter for serious concern.

These disappointments do not appear to deter States from planning. On the contrary, Mali is preparing to plan more

TABLE 1. School enrolment rates by level of education around 1960 and 1970

Major regions	Percentage of children of primary school age enrolled in an educational establishment		Percentage of children of secondary school age enrolled in an educational establishment		Percentage of children of primary or secondary school age enrolled in an educational establishment		Percentage of students enrolled in education at the third level, as a ratio of the population aged between 20 and 24 years	
	Around 1960	Around 1970	Around 1960	Around 1970	Around 1960	Around 1970	Around 1960	Around 1970
Total world[a]	63	71	32	54	50	63	6.0	11.0
Africa	34	48	12	25	24	38	0.8	1.5
North America	98	99	90	93	94	97	30.2	48.2
Latin America	60	78	26	49	45	65	3.1	6.3
Asia[a]	50	59	22	44	36	55	2.6	4.9
Europe and USSR	96	97	57	67	79	85	8.6	17.0
Oceania	95	97	60	75	80	89	10.0	14.0
(Arab States)	(38)	(61)	(16)	(28)	(28)	(45)	(2.1)	(4.0)

a. Excluding the People's Republic of China, the Democratic People's Republic of Korea and the Democratic Republic of Vietnam.

Source: Office of Statistics, Unesco.

systematically, establishing a strict admission percentage for each level of study ; the enrolment rate at the first level of basic education, for children between seven and twelve years of age, will be kept at 20 per cent ; 35 per cent of the sixth year pupils will be admitted to the second level ; 66 per cent of those graduating from basic education will be able to gain admission to secondary education. In order to supplement this enrolment effort and to offset the shortfall it implies, Mali plans to undertake a simultaneous strengthening of informal educational activities.

It would therefore appear that planning is not on the decline in the Third World, although illusions are a thing of the past and it is no longer taken for granted that planned education is necessarily education adapted to the needs of society.

The most highly industrialized States have their own problems. In the United States, for example, where there is a generally-held belief in the virtues of economic efficiency and performance, it has been noted that a large number of young people graduate from secondary schools or even from college without a clear idea of what job they are going to do and without having received any directly relevant training. Yet at the same time, industry is having the greatest difficulty in filling vacant posts. It is an awareness of this two-fold inadequacy on the part of schools that led France, the Federal Republic of Germany and the United Kingdom, for example, to contemplate radical reforms.

But to what extent are planners justified in making education subject to the demands of the economy ? Or, to present the problem in more topical terms, how far can the overriding interest of society be equated with the desire for productivity ? These questions are certainly not new, and the age-old debate on the ultimate goals of education is unlikely to produce any answers in the near future. However, at a time when the consumer society is being challenged so radically, one may well wonder whether it is right to regard the child and adolescent as future producers. In situations as critical as that of Cuba, where both the survival of the national economy and the building of a new society are at stake, heroic solutions such as that of enrolling school pupils into the labour force are admissable. However respectful and, no doubt, effective such solutions may be, they are nevertheless not a valid model for the rest of the world.

This question was well formulated by the delegate of Hungary at the most recent International Conference of Education. Without disputing that there should be the closest possible relationship between education and manpower requirements, he pointed out that estimates of these requirements could not be the sole basis for educational planning. Estimates often turn out to be inaccurate, and any error, far from promoting economic expansion, is likely to paralyse it. For this reason, in a resolution adopted in June 1972, the Central Committee of the Hungarian Communist Party came out in favour of planning which allowed simultaneously for the economic, social and cultural needs of the nation. The objective of education would not be to train young people merely to carry out specific functions in the economic sphere but also, and above all, to assume personal and collective responsibilities on the basis of a thorough understanding of the techniques used in the economy and the ways of life which the economy tends to impose on society in the normal course of events.

It is, indeed, within this frame of reference that discussion concerning educational adaptation should take place. Whatever the political régime, no system of education, if it is to be true to its calling, can take the improvement of productivity as its goal. It is equally true that development, if it is to justify the hopes which people place in it, cannot be measured in terms of economic expansion or national income ; what is the point of increasing the material resources of a country if such action fails to bring about progress in social justice and individual liberty or to offer any new prospects of happiness ? The function of an education which is adapted to current needs is, surely, as it has always been, concerned with 'learning to be', to use a recent and already celebrated phrase or, as a poet has said, 'learning the job of living, a hard and worthy trade'.

The cost of education

No progress is possible in education without heavy financial outlay. As early as 1968, Philip H. Coombs pointed to the rapid rise in the cost of education as the precursor of an impending crisis ; in his view, the time was coming when no country would be able to continue increasing its public expenditure in this field and when the governments would be faced with a dramatic choice between the expansion of education and that of other equally deserving social sectors. Has this time already come ? The share of education in the budget of many highly industrialized States is tending to level off, just as it is in the distribution of national income. But, although the Federal Government of the United States, as has already been stated, points out the serious difficulties raised by the financing of public education, it is not certain that the most highly developed countries have already reached, or will shortly reach, the critical point anticipated by Philip H. Coombs. Yet the countries of the Third World are sounding a note of alarm : Dahomey for example, where expenditure on education increased by 40 per cent between 1965 and 1970, and which already devotes 29 per cent of the State budget to education—or Ghana, Mali, Thailand and Zaire. Beautiful illusions now seem to belong to the past. There is no longer any question of the majority of African countries achieving the Addis Ababa objectives, for many of them will have difficulty in maintaining their present school enrolment even at its still very low level.

If expansion, the *sine qua non* of democratization, is proving difficult, what hope can there be of improving the quality of education ? The United States report mentions the generally recognized principle that a good education is more expensive than a bad one. Although it is difficult to specify what constitutes a good education, it is hardly logical to claim that education is being provided in satisfactory conditions if the necessary premises, equipment and teaching staff are not available. No doubt imagination or experience may suggest ingenious expedients, such as using the same school premises for two groups of pupils, one shift working in the morning and the other in the afternoon, creating mobile teams of teachers serving several villages in rotation, using any available building such as a church, a temple or a mosque for teaching purposes, or following the Cuban example of cross-age teaching, whereby older pupils are made responsible for teaching the younger ones. Each of these approaches is, indeed, used in various countries as can be seen from the national reports submitted to Unesco. There are even countries in which the poverty of families makes it incumbent on the State to pay not only for the transport of pupils, a practice which is becoming fairly general, but also for their food and clothing. These are yet further expenses that must be added to existing ones.

This being so, how is one to provide for improved methods and techniques ? Everyone is aware that even the slightest innovation is expensive, but standardized or pre-fabricated premises do not readily lend themselves to independent work by pupils, streaming by ability or individualized forms of teaching. And what of audio-visual facilities ? Although Niger has carried out successful experiments in this respect, and although Ivory Coast provides an example almost without parallel anywhere in the world of primary education given mainly by television, a large amount of outside assistance was required in both personnel and equipment, an effort in which international co-operation blends harmoniously with bilateral aid. But outside assistance from whatever source is never entirely free ; as long as it continues it imposes fairly heavy burdens on the recipient countries and, as soon as it ends, such countries bear the entire burden alone. For the Third World, far more than for developed nations, improved teaching methods, which are a determining factor in providing better education, often appear to be a luxury.

The main problem in the financing of education is that of teachers. Although, by a strange paradox, the United States has an alarming surplus of qualified teachers (to such an extent that, if the present rate continues, it is anticipated that a million qualified teachers will be unemployed in 1980), and although in industrialized countries the shortage of teaching staff now seems to have been overcome, the problem remains extremely acute in a large number of developing countries. The shortage is due not only to inadequate recruitment but also to the poor qualifications of teachers. Moreover, all countries are conscious of a need to improve teacher training and this is high on the list of urgent problems enumerated in national reports, not only in Argentina, Dahomey, Egypt, the Libyan Arab Republic, the Syrian Arab Republic, Thailand, and Zaire, but also in Belgium, France, the Federal Republic of Germany, the United Kingdom and the Soviet Union. In some cases the problem is one of improving initial training, and in others it is a matter of providing further training for teachers already employed.

No satisfactory solution has yet been found for this second

aspect of the problem, that of retraining. France has admittedly granted primary school-teachers the right to improvement courses, but it will be many years before all teachers have had the opportunity to attend such courses ; the United Kingdom plans to grant its own teachers special leave every five years to enable them to take refresher courses, and in the Soviet Union large numbers of advanced training centres have been established, in addition to correspondence courses. Moreover, the Soviet Union, like Poland, recently announced measures to raise the salaries of teachers and to improve their working conditions.

Such changes are welcome and will inevitably help to improve education. But, together with all the other expenses, they increase still further a financial burden which is beyond the means of all but a rather limited number of countries. Nothing is more difficult for a government than to calculate accurately the total cost of education for the country as a whole. The budget of the Ministry of Education is only a partial indication ; in addition one should take into consideration the budgets of a large number of other sectors which contribute, often to a considerable extent, to specialized education, vocational training, adult education, or general health and school medical services—not to speak of the direct or indirect contributions of regional or local bodies. Moreover, such expenditure covers only contributions from public funds ; the voluntary or statutory participation of commercial firms, like the contribution of religious communities or private bodies, are often impossible to estimate accurately. In spite of the studies which have already been made of the subject, educational financing still comprises large areas of uncertainty. [1]

Even the systematic studies carried out in certain countries lend themselves to varying interpretations. It has, for example, been calculated that the annual cost of education in the United Kingdom between 1950 and 1963 rose from £50 to £150 per pupil. According to the authors of this survey, the increase is due to an improvement in quality ; another economist, however, using the same data but a more refined method of calculation, reaches the

1. See especially : Vaizey, J. ; Chesswas, J.D. *The costing of educational plans*. Paris, Unesco : IIEP, 1969. 63 p. See also : Coombs, P.H. ; Hallak, J. *Educational cost analysis*. Paris, Unesco : IIEP, 1972. 3 vols.

conclusion that the difference was due mainly to over-all price inflation [47].[1]

Nevertheless, the results of such studies are extremely useful not only because of the reliability of their information but above all for the practical conclusions that governments can draw from them. The problems of improving education without excessive expense presents governments with a major task. Those who suggest workable solutions, or even possible lines of approach, will earn the gratitude of mankind. Judging by a document published recently by the Council of Europe,[2] Sweden, whose system of education is regarded as exemplary, seems to offer some grounds for hope : no doubt it is a subjective assessment which has not so far been verified by a cost-effectiveness study, but a Swedish report states that 'research has provided a means of increasing efficiency without unduly increasing costs' and that 'in certain fields it has even been possible to reduce expenditure'. Thus, notwithstanding the well-known axiom, it seems possible that a good education might cost no more than a bad one. This is indeed welcome news and it is very much to be hoped that this research will be pursued so that other countries may make use of it ; for if any topic should be a matter of international co-operation, it is surely this one.

Abiding and, in many cases, worsening problems, painstaking research, the likelihood of solutions, an unbroken succession of reforms, constant changes and universal, but as yet poorly co-ordinated, efforts are the features which, judging from pronouncements on the subject, appear to be characteristic of educational development throughout the world.

1. The figures in square brackets refer to the bibliographical references at the end of this volume.

2. This document was issued in 1973 under the symbol DECS/Rech. (73).

Chapter two

Secondary education, training and employment

It is certainly a sign of the times that the governments of Unesco's Member States should have chosen the relationship between education, training and employment at the level of secondary education as the special theme of an international conference of ministries of education. Barely twenty years ago one would not have conceived of the idea, or it would have been rejected as too daring. Economists at that time were busy exploring the possible cause and effect relationship between the development of education and the economic process, and between the full use of human resources and rising living standards. Following the example of the socialist States, they were recommending relatively flexible educational planning based on society's needs. It is, nevertheless, still a recent idea that there might be a structural and even necessary connexion between the extension of education and the creation of new jobs or, inversely, between the labour market and the slant given to education, and this is what suggested the word 'relationship' chosen for the subject of the Conference. It is a proposition which even today lends itself to much discussion, especially among ministers of education. The subject to be explored is so vast and touches on so many different fields that one may well wonder whether the authorities responsible for education are qualified to tackle it.

In their preparatory work, Unesco and IBE therefore called on experts from other international organizations, such as the International Labour Organisation (ILO) and the United Nations Food and Agriculture Organization (FAO), as well as on private assistance. For their part, Member States had to give the matter thorough consideration and carry out studies, the findings of which are contained in the national reports submitted to the Conference. Without underestimating the importance of the discussions held at Geneva, or the significance of the final recommendations, it may be said that what made the Conference in the autumn of 1973 so memorable an occasion was, above all, the amount of information and observations that were assembled at that time.[1] It was certainly the first time that the question had been studied on such a vast scale all over the world.

THE ELEMENTS OF THE PROPOSITION

Each of the three terms contributing to the title of this chapter calls for a few introductory remarks. It might well be asked why the field was limited to *secondary education*, and whether it would not have been more natural to include or to start with higher education. Universities have been training students for careers in medicine, the legal professions or teaching for centuries. More recently, this type of training was supplemented, in the universities themselves or in other equivalent institutions, by the training of senior-level staff for industry, agriculture, commerce and public or private administration. The relationships between higher education and vocational training have long been obvious, even if not always satisfactory. In secondary education, however, the situation is more obscure, experience still recent and the direction to be followed less obvious. It was possibly the difficulty of the task and, above all, its novelty that influenced the choice. Perhaps the role of the State was also borne in mind, since this is more apparent at the secondary level than in the universities which are recognized as independent in many countries. Moreover, secondary education was better suited to international comparisons of national policies. However, we never lost sight of the fact that the relationships between education, training and employment do not cease at the end of secondary education, as our study will shortly demonstrate.

Although the term secondary education is current in inter-

1. The reports submitted by Member States in response to the questionnaire may be consulted at the IBE in Geneva. They have also been reproduced on microfiches as part of the Unesco : IBE SIRE collection.

national usage, we should bear in mind that it is used to describe structures which differ greatly from country to country. In one, a distinction is made between two successive stages in secondary education, in another, the first of these stages is linked with primary grades to form a single system and in yet others, it forms a self-contained intermediate stage. To avoid any confusion, however, it has been agreed that by secondary education is meant education intended for the age-group from 11 to 12 to about 17 or 18 years of age.

There is a great deal of ambiguity about the concept of *training*. Much is often said about character training as the major goal of education, and by this is meant a process which is both intellectual, physical and moral and which permits the development of all the faculties of the child or adolescent. In the present instance, however, where a distinction is made between training and education, the term is obviously attributed a more specific and restricted meaning. Are we to accept the idea proposed by the Geneva Conference that 'there is a specificity in the term "training", the notion of preparation of particular skills for the exercise of a particular occupation' ? And since we are talking about secondary education, should we agree to confine ourselves to 'systems directed to middle-level occupations, for qualified skilled workers or technicians' ? To do so would, at first sight, seem to exclude, in favour of industry, other sectors of the economy such as agriculture and the vast tertiary sector. It would also imply turning a blind eye to the other purposes of training at the secondary level, such as the preparation of students for further training as higher-level personnel. We should avoid the pitfalls of an unduly rigid compartmentalization and agree, at the outset, that what is meant by training is vocational training of any kind.

It must nevertheless be admitted that the narrow definition which, for the moment, we have rejected at least had the advantage of introducing the third element of the problem, namely, *employment*. Here again we come up against a complex idea. It intimidates educators, who rarely have occasion to deal with it, and specialists have considerable difficulty in coming to terms with it. Some twenty years ago, in accordance with the idea of certain experts, it was widely believed that the lack of employment opportunities was the result of too insufficient economic growth, and that an expanding economy would expand the labour market in the same proportions. Nevertheless, it is obvious today that these hopes have not been realized. In many countries of the Third World, where economic development has made significant progress, employment remains in a critical position. It is this situation which led the International Labour Organisation, in its World Employment Programme, to draw the attention of Member States to the specific nature of the aims that must be embodied in a consistent policy in respect of employment [4e].

Unemployment is a valuable indicator in this connexion. In Sri Lanka, for example, 92 per cent of the young persons who obtained their secondary school certificate after at least ten years of education, are unable to find employment. Some 64 per cent of the 20-24 age group are still unemployed, and the lack of adaptation of secondary education to the needs of the labour market has assumed critical proportions in this country. In Peru where the ILO has carried out similar studies, the evil tends to take the form of under-employment, since although the rate of visible unemployment among young graduates does not appear at all alarming, many of them are in fact obliged to take jobs very much inferior to their qualifications, offering a wage which is barely equal to the legal minimum. Employers, for their part, emboldened by the strength of the demand, require of candidates a level of education far higher than that actually needed. This situation has, in fact, made the Peruvian Government decide to reform the education system completely.

Another item of information made available by the ILO, but this time about Kenya, reveals that, on completion of their secondary school education, young people refuse to take on farm work and crowd into the towns to seek jobs which they feel are more 'modern', but which the economy has been unable to create in sufficient numbers. What these young people want from school, more than applicable knowledge and skills, are diplomas which in turn could open the door to specific kinds of employment and certain scales of remuneration.

From a strictly economic point of view, we are eventually obliged to ask whether the rapid extension of secondary education has not been a bad investment for many developing countries. Would it not have been wiser to invest more in creating new employment opportunities instead of opening so many secondary schools and colleges ? Men or women with a modest elementary education but more certain of finding work would surely have been more useful and even happier than people with a school certificate who are condemned to unemployment or under-employment. A detailed study of agricultural conditions in tropical regions has led certain FAO experts to question the effectiveness of education as a tool of development unless it is made part of an over-all policy, which should also include a reform of the land tenure system, and an expansion of credit facilities and markets for produce. In the absence of an integrated development policy, these experts fear that the expansion of education might even have the effect of creating more difficulties than it helps solve. In their view young people who have been educated but are unable to take advantage in their work life of the knowledge and skills learned at school are beginning to pose for the Third World 'a problem fraught with as many dangers as illiteracy' [4d].

This thought might well sound shocking to educators convinced of the intrinsic virtues of education. It has not been proved, in any case, that economists are always right, for they, too, are guilty of errors of judgement and particularly errors of prediction. Even in the recent past many have had to change their views and contradict themselves. Yet, those whose sombre predictions have just been mentioned were not blaming education itself ; what they were questioning was the system adopted by a large number of developing countries which patterned themselves on the most highly developed States.

Here again, what is being condemned is the fact that education is ill-adapted to requirements, is unable to prepare young people for the life that they will lead later on in their natural and social environment, and unable to provide them with productive and remunerative work, and to assure their happiness and a place in the community. But regardless whether one opts for educational reform or, if necessary, the non-formal types of education which are being developed in Africa, Asia or Latin America through the bold use of audio-visual aids, as in Dahomey, India or Mexico, the main thing is to bear in mind the words so often used by René Dumont that 'Agricultural development, particularly in the tropics, requires the complete re-shaping of education'.

EDUCATION POLICIES
AND EMPLOYMENT POLICIES

The other lesson to be learnt from these examples is that even
a bold education policy cannot by itself solve the problem of
development. During the 1950s the work of certain economists
demonstrated that education was capable of making a major
contribution to economic expansion. In the great surge of enthusiasm which, at that time, enveloped the international organizations and, subsequently, the countries of the Third World, plans
as ambitious as they were courageous, such as the Addis
Ababa Plan for Africa and the Karachi Plan for South-East Asia,
were drawn up for the development of education. The education
budget in every country began to rise, absorbing an ever greater
share of the national income. Today the euphoria is over. Some
plans proved impossible to achieve, the rapid development of
education was not followed by any rise in levels of living and now
unemployment and under-employment is rife among young people,
despite their diplomas. Yet is this a reason for condemning education ? The mass movement in the direction of centres of education
reflects an irreversible trend just as powerful as the right of everyone to education. This fact cannot be disregarded by any government in the world. Although economics has its own laws, it is
now a generally recognized fact that human progress calls for
universal education.

What people failed to realize or fully appreciate was that
development requires integrated policies which can influence all
economic and social factors, including education. At that
level—the highest national level—the responsibility is borne col-
lectively by the government as a whole. But to what extent are
ministers of education really associated with the preparation of
national development policies and particularly with arrangements
made concerning the labour market ? To what extent are their
departments aware of these matters ? In other words, are there
any channels of communication between education and the
working world ? The International Conference on Education had
to consider all these questions at its thirty-fourth session and, in
order to enable the Conference to discuss them in an informed way,
Unesco first put these questions to its Member States.

Some countries have found constructive answers. The socialist countries head the list because, for them, the planning of education forms an integral part of an over-all economic, social and cultural development policy. Interesting details on this subject are to be found in the reports submitted by Bulgaria, Cuba, Czechoslovakia and Yugoslavia, for each of these countries has adopted a solution corresponding to its circumstances. Several Arab States, and particularly Egypt, seem to be following the same path, as is also Afghanistan. As part of its plan for 1971-1975, the Argentine Republic has prepared a bold reform which, as we have seen, embraces all the various stages of education, vocational training at all levels, and the preparation of young people for productive work. Canada, where economic planning and employment questions are a federal concern while education is under the jurisdiction of the provincial authorities, has a Review and Assessment Committee consisting of representatives of the Federal Department of Manpower and the Departments of Education in each province. A similar desire for co-ordination led to the establishment of the Vocational Training Council in New Zealand. Japan's education authorities participate in the work of the Employment Council and the Central Vocational Training Council. In France, the 1971 laws on continuous training confer the power of initiative in this field on the Minister of Education.

In other countries, for which such precise information is not available, it is not clear whether the national or regional education authorities are associated with economic planning or employment policy matters. In these circumstances, the education sector is reduced to finding its own way, guided by its own experience and research, or on the basis of its forecasts of population trends or public demand. Lack of communication and even distrust between educators and teachers on the one hand and economists on the other are the inevitable results of this situation. Educators and teachers complain that economists are encroaching on their preserves, that they are unfamiliar with the processes peculiar to education and are attempting to make them conform to an alien context, whereas economists accuse educators and teachers of remaining in splendid isolation, thereby prolonging the dangerous inadequacies of education. In order to bring each side closer to the other in the interests of a joint effort and to put an end to this absurd misunderstanding, Unesco has for several years taken the initiative in convening periodic conferences in each of the major regions of the world, attended not only by the ministers of education but also by the ministers responsible for economic planning in the participating States. During 1971, for example, the Caracas Conference for Latin America and the Singapore Conference for Asia thus took place within a few months of one another. The list of participants admittedly reveals a serious imbalance, numerically at least, between the two categories of participants, as these conferences were attended by far more ministers of education than ministers of economic affairs. Yet, even if the immediate impact of these conferences was limited, the idea behind them is certainly sound and may one day produce the desired results.

THE ORGANIZATION
OF VOCATIONAL TRAINING

In passing on from this survey of policies to an examination of the organization of studies, one is immediately struck by the immense variety of structures not only in different States but also within one and the same country. This diversity has a historical explanation and justification, for throughout history all human societies have made some kind of arrangement to train young people for their active life, whether within the family, the clan or tribe, or within a certain profession. What is known as apprenticeship has invariably been the subject of individual or collective attention in the community under the guidance of an elder or mentor, employer or business manager, in accordance with customary practice in agriculture, the handicraft sector or industry. Each people has inherited a system of this kind, which has left its mark on even the most developed societies and the most complex systems.

Unesco's survey shows that no State shirks its responsibility for training young people to prepare them for a career ; national legislation in this sphere is constantly being expanded and improved. As regulations were extended to the international level, a body of conventions or recommendations came into being, the initiative for which originated with the International Labour

Organisation. The diversity apparent in national systems is not a reflection of the amount of attention paid by various countries to these problems but rather of the diversity of customs they have inherited and of the measures they have adapted in recent times, depending on their political systems, their social structure, their level of economic development, their cultural characteristics or their concept of the function of education. It is extremely revealing in this respect to compare available histories of education and the histories of the organization of labour.

Traditional handicraft customs, true to their old-fashioned picturesque forms, still persist in some countries of Western Europe, especially in certain trades such as carpentry. Large industrial firms established their own apprenticeship and training schemes long ago, but they have also for long been criticized for following selfish motives, providing only for their own needs and restricting their pupils to narrow specializations which are subject to the vicissitudes of economic circumstances. However the State and the trade unions were not slow in taking action, with the result that in France, for example, a state technical and vocational training section was established at the beginning of this century, its cost and management being shared by the State, firms, and employers' and workers' associations through an extraordinarily complicated network of institutions. It took many years and a series of reforms to co-ordinate, simplify and unify this system and to bring it into line with the requirements of modern education.

At the time that colonial territories abandoned customary education and adapted imported forms of education at the instigation of the metropolitan power, agricultural or industrial undertakings were still too weak to take on the burden of even a rudimentary form of education. In the former colonies, since their accession to independence, it is therefore the State, through a national education policy, which has provided the bulk of vocational training for young people, A perusal of the national reports quite clearly confirms that this sector of education is of constant concern in most countries of the Third World, and that the extremely urgent need for its adaptation is making itself felt. The sections on training in these reports are replete with all the usual problems, such as the improvement of training, equality of opportunity for children from towns and rural areas and for girls and boys, the search for an education system suited to the circumstances of the rural environment, and the elimination of illiteracy, unemployment and under-employment. And as people are beginning to realize that the school will be unable to satisfy all these needs, they are turning with great expectations towards the training aspects of non-formal types of education.

In the developed countries where vocational training already has a long history, two broad categories can be distinguished depending on the role assigned to State education. In the United Kingdom, for example, vocational training is the responsibility of boards which were set up in 1964, whose members consist of employers and employees as well as officials from the education services. Thus, although State education bodies have not been left out in the cold, they do not play the most important part on these boards and are not responsible for them. In socialist countries such as Bulgaria, on the other hand, it is the responsibility of the Ministry of Education to provide training in all sectors of employment. Technical and vocational training in France has been the concern of the Ministry of Education for many years. Legislation recently adopted in Denmark and Norway has the effect of making training the responsibility of educational establishments and not of firms through their apprenticeship schemes.

Both systems have their advantages and disadvantages. For example, it is readily admitted that training provided at school, being removed from the strictly utilitarian concerns of business, takes account not only of the interests of the pupil but also those of the community and strikes the right balance between general education and specific preparation for a trade. On the other hand, there is a danger that training offered at school will be less practical and less effective and, as it entails costly equipment and a large number of staff with a variety of skills, it imposes crushing burdens on the State.

For these reasons, some countries have chosen a third, middle, path which makes it possible to take advantage of both the resources of school and those of firms in that the apprenticeship is done at school. The State remains responsible for them throughout the compulsory schooling period but, by means of a contract, entrusts duly selected public or private firms with the task of providing practical job-oriented training. This alternation of education and apprenticeship may assume various forms. In the Federal Republic of Germany, for example, the working week is split between apprenticeship training and school. In New Brunswick, Canada, the apprentices go back to school each year for a three- to six-week training course. In Czechoslovakia, on the other hand, apprenticeship training alternates between centres set up within firms and State apprenticeship schools. The advantage of these various approaches is their great flexibility, which permits full use to be made of available premises, equipment and staff and ensures prudent housekeeping.

THE NATURE OF TRAINING

It is really only of secondary importance whether training is the monopoly of the State, or is provided at centres distinct from government schools, or is made available on the basis of co-operation between schools and firms. Education cannot and must not strive for uniformity, since the bonds linking it to society, the environment, the political régime and cultural traditions are too intimate. What is important in training, as in all matters connected with education, is that the subjects taught should correspond to requirements.

So far, we have considered only the specifically vocational nature of training or, in other words, according to the definition which we have provisionally adopted, 'the acquisition of particular skills for the exercise of a particular occupation'. From this point of view, the effectiveness of training is judged by its ability to lead directly on to a trade. Taken to extremes, there should therefore be as many special kinds of training as there are trades. This is, in fact, what would happen if firms alone were responsible for apprenticeship, since each one wishes to obtain the skilled workers it requires within the strict limits of its own needs. A report on vocational education, prepared in Denmark in 1971, mentioned the existence of more than 150 different kinds of training for an equal number of trades. In its desire for specialization, the French Ministry of Education in the recent past also used to issue a vast range of certificates of professional aptitude, each of which was valid only for one trade. The disadvantages of this system soon became evident, since it failed to make any provision for rapid changes in production techniques, created the danger either of unemployment or manpower shortage, and did not offer job mobility or promotion to those who had supposedly been trained. In addition, specialization early in life never manages to satisfy all the requirements of industry. The Czechoslovak Minister of Education certainly had a point when he reminded firms that 'the role of the education system is to provide general training which matches the needs of a particular branch of industry— mechanical engineering, for example, or construction—but not the needs of a specific factory'. The crux of the problem here is to situate training at the right level, so that it can adapt itself to fluc- tuations in the labour market or changes in technology and yet ensure the full development of the faculties of each individual.

At this stage of our analysis, a new distinction must be intro- duced. In international usage, there is frequent confusion between the concepts of vocational training and technical education. In the English-speaking countries, the term 'technical' is generally used only of the highest level of education, and we hear of colleges of advanced technology or even technical universities. At other levels, the term 'polytechnic' is used to describe the basic, ten-year education. In France and other French-speaking countries, on the other hand, a technical education is one of the options offered during the second stage of secondary education to students of about 15 to 18 years of age. The idea is nevertheless the same, and the main distinguishing feature of technical education is not so much its objective as its content. Technical studies are based on the technological applications of science and although they may vary in level they invariably include workshop practice. They all certainly point to careers in industry, agriculture, commerce or management, but do not necessarily assure students of employment. In other words (and this is where they differ from vocational train- ing), there may be openings at the end of secondary education for technicians or skilled workers, although advanced studies at a university of a specialized institute may be required. Technical education offers a general acquaintance with broad areas of techno- logy rather than a practical specialization.

Nevertheless, despite the vast prospects it opens up, this educa- tion does not attract the most gifted or most ambitious pupils. Even in the most industrialized countries, it is a victim of deep-rooted social prejudice. A glance at the reports from Denmark and Finland is particularly revealing in this respect. It is a well-known fact that in France itself, the 'grandes écoles', which give access to top jobs in industry, in most cases recruit their students from the science classes of secondary schools rather than the technical classes. Most governments are at one in their wish to combat this prejudice, improve the calibre of candidates admitted and raise the level of studies in technical education—and many recent reforms have precisely this aim in view. In France, one and the same certificate, the *baccalaureat,* is now awarded at the end of secondary education for classical or modern studies, as well as for technological subjects. Yet prejudices persist, particularly if technical education is provided in schools different from the others. The solution adopted by countries like Sweden or the United Kingdom thus seems both the simplest and the most effective. The 'new gymnasium' in Sweden and the British comprehensive school admit pupils of the same age group into one and the same establishment and provide a complete range of secondary level courses—classical, technical, industrial and commercial. The idea of the comprehensive school has already been adopted in other countries such as Canada, and is gaining ground in Belgium, Denmark, Egypt, Finland, Ghana, Iraq and Nigeria. Its future is clearly most promising.

Yet even improved school structures are not enough to overcome all difficulties. Within one and the same school, certain prejudices may persist about subjects which are reputed to be less desirable than others. With a view to overcoming psychological barriers, informing young people of existing possibilities and making it easier for them to choose the path they are to follow, the programmes recently adopted in France for the first stage of secondary education include an introduction to technology for the third and fourth years (children of about 13 or 14 years of age) which is compulsory. The aim of this course is to provide students with a better understanding of the nature of modern technology and to stimulate a taste for practical work. As considerable initiative is left to the teachers, who are usually physicists, the initial results were not always satisfactory.

There has been hesitation over the choice of methods, ideas themselves have changed and research is being conducted on the subject. A path has nevertheless been opened up which may lead to something much more than the manual work of bygone days. Several countries such as Egypt, Jordan or Madagascar also seem to have adopted the idea of an introduction to technology.

GUIDANCE

All this research, these experiments and changes are designed to assist students in choosing between the various options offered by secondary education, such as arts or science, general or technical education, studies leading to higher education, or vocational training for direct access to employment. Educators are clearly paying increasing attention to the problem of guidance. As part of its present reform, the Federal Republic of Germany, like several other European States before it, has just introduced a two-year 'orientation' period at the beginning of secondary education, which will become compulsory from 1976. The forms and methods of this 'orientation' may vary from country to country, but there is agreement on a certain number of conditions which should be met in all cases :

1.   Specialization should not take place too early. It generally occurs about the age of 15 after an initial period of basic studies, which should be the same for all children, in order to promote equality of opportunity. Even 15 is too early an age for some educators. The reform currently being carried out in Yugoslavia extends general education by two years. 'Through the two years' prolongation', it says in the report submitted by Yugoslavia, 'the possibility is given to the student of making a more mature decision on his future vocation.' Nevertheless, there are also disadvantages in unduly postponing specialization, and the findings of some United States experts indicate that such postponement has very little effect on the choices already made by students. Most education systems, as well as the labour market, have difficulty in coping with late specialization.

2.   Generally speaking, specialization within the school is of significance to the school itself, since it facilitates and shapes the choice between the various options offered by secondary education, such as arts, science or technology. Yet it should be

borne in mind that, in selecting a particular specialization, the pupil is taking a decision that will, to a large extent, affect his future. Either he will start work on completion of his secondary education (and in this case it is important that he leaves school with qualifications giving him access to employment) or he will go on to higher education, and in this case it is not as important for him to have chosen the path best suited to his abilities. For all these reasons, specialization always has implications for a person's future employment and must therefore be based on as much information as possible about careers and career prospect. If the school authorities are unable to supply this information, appropriate specialized services should be established in each region. This results in a complex system involving specially trained teachers, psychologists and advisers, as well as experienced documentalists. Not all countries, however, are in a position to set up a costly organization of this nature.

3. In countries where the planning of education is fully integrated with economic development plans, specialization is mandatory, and pupils and their families have no option but to conform to the system. In this way the desired balance is achieved between the various kinds of training and courses offered. In other countries, guidance takes the form of specific suggestions, and those who refuse to follow them are required to take further tests, the results of which are decisive. In some cases nothing more than simple advice is offered, but it is questionable whether this is still tantamount to forcing a student to follow a certain direction. Social prejudice is given free reign. In any case, the advantages and disadvantages of various systems depend on political régimes or national policy considerations much more than on considerations of an educational nature.

What matters above all is that guidance must not assume a negative aspect, for then it is equivalent to selection, a word abhorred by large numbers of young people because of its undertones of disappointment, bitterness and frustration. Constructive guidance, even if it has the effect of barring certain avenues to the student, must be based first and foremost on usable skills and genuine prospects ; it must point to the chances of success, even if at a more modest level than has been hoped, rather than to the risks of failure.

4. This means that specialization must be the result of broad co-operation not only between those who bring their skills to bear on the problem and between these experts and the families of students, but above all with the young people who are less directly concerned. Students must not have guidance imposed on them but must feel that they are playing an active part in it. In preparing the documents necessary for the discussions on education, training and employment, the International Bureau of Education had the excellent idea of asking an assistant at the Ecole de psychologie et des sciences de l'éducation at the University of Geneva to undertake a critical study of recent work on the hopes of young people for their future. This document he called 'Young people's attitudes to school, the adult world and employment' [4g]. After elucidating the causes of a profoundly critical attitude towards education systems, the report summarizing the conclusions of the survey ends with these words : 'A radically new form of training must be given to young people so that they can discover the means of choosing their path in accordance with their own aspirations and not in accordance with those which others think they have or would like them to have .... Whatever the prevailing conditions and the opportunities offered by the education system, no one with responsibility for the training of the young ought to forget that the latter can situate themselves in relation to their training or their future only if the governance of their schooling and vocational training is in their own hands, i.e. if they become effectively responsible for it.' Young people will certainly always need information and advice, but schools and educators should make it possible for students to become conscious and active partners in the difficult process of finding their path and for the resulting choice to be genuinely theirs. In most cases, this requires really radical changes.

5. Last, but by no means least, the choice of specialization made at school must never be considered as final. Errors are always possible and always will be, but as soon as they are discovered it should be possible to correct them at any time during the student's subsequent education. The choice of another course

is possible only if there are sufficient 'bridges' between the various courses offered at the secondary level so that a student who has made a wrong choice can change his direction without suffering thereby. The most developed education systems certainly make provision for such 'bridges' so that these transfers are possible in theory, but it is only too well known how many obstacles the rigidity of structures creates and how much it jeopardizes the chances of success. Here also much progress remains to be made towards greater flexibility and mobility.

EDUCATION AND WORK

The school environment rarely enables students to form a very balanced and accurate idea of working life and employment in general. Education systems have developed throughout history with the aim of meeting their own needs and satisfying requirements essentially educational in nature. It was for long considered advisable to keep education sheltered from unsettling outside influences and protected against the shocks of everyday life. Now that it has had to yield to external pressures and become more open, it is often criticized for becoming the favourite and very vulnerable battleground of conflicting political passions. All the same, whether education has become a political football or not, it remains aloof from the harsh realities of productive work. How can a pupil who is wrapped up in his work or exposed to the influence of ideas whose significance he does not always understand, form an accurate picture of the job which he will later take on and the working conditions which await him? Specialization, with its dual educational and employment implications, can be successful only if the world of the school is opened up fully to the world of employment.

This was the purpose of the measures recently adopted in France to enable all teachers to attend long training courses in large firms in the hope that the experience they acquire by participating in active work of a completely different kind, would benefit them personally, and assist them in their teaching and in their relationship with their students.

Other countries with a similar aim in view are casting about for new formulae to be applied in their secondary schools. Mention should be made of a particularly interesting experiment which has been going on for several years in certain parts of the United States. Surveys had shown that a large number of young Americans left school or even completed their first years of higher education without giving any thought to their future career and without acquiring skills that could be used directly in productive work. The idea thus arose of establishing a new kind of school combining primary and secondary education and the three kinds of programmes which had previously been used, namely, general education, vocational education and university preparation. The general education offered in these new schools is the same as in any other school but at the same time provides real career guidance and, depending on the student's choice, enables him either to start working immediately or to go on to higher education. They are, therefore, a kind of comprehensive school, their programmes being the same for all pupils and preparing them all for active life.

In the initial stages, the principal aim is to help children become aware of the nature and conditions of work in a large number of jobs, divided into groups so as to facilitate the way they are presented. In the second stage, the students themselves choose two or three groups of jobs for closer study. This is the time for job exploration, but no choice is yet final. After this comes the third and final stage, during which they receive real training that will assure them of employment in the field they have selected. General education is at no time sacrificed to training and although, when they leave these schools, all these young people are qualified for a particular job, they are nevertheless able, if they so desire, to continue their education in one of the branches of higher education. No system is perfect, and this one has been in existence too short a time for any opinion to be expressed about its success. However, it offers the prospect of a truly comprehensive education in which the requirements of a good general education are reconciled with those of graded and active specialization, and which also opens wide a window onto the actual circumstances of productive work. This is perhaps one of the approaches that will be used in the future.

Much more radical and more ambitious is the general law on education promulgated in Peru in 1972, since it tends to break down all barriers between the school and its environment. Instead of remaining entrenched within its walls, as in the quite recent past, forming an enclave in the surrounding community, the new school will be mananged by the community, thus benefiting from all its resources and rendering maximum services in return, with the participation and to the advantage of the entire population. A community school run by the community for the community would seem to offer yet another possibility for the future.

The People's Republic of China, which entered Unesco officially only at the end of 1972, has not yet made a very active contribution to the Organization's work. The only information we have about China therefore comes from a non-official source. What is known about the reform of the education system brought in by the cultural revolution, nevertheless suggests that it is designed to create conditions for 'the most complete interdependence' of every teaching unit (at all levels from primary to higher education) and the socio-economic collective on which it depends, in such a way that one and the same spirit quickens productive work on the one hand and, on the other, the new culture that is forming. Participation in work is a fundamental discipline for the pupils. In a school in Songshu in Liaoning, 'all kinds of work whereby school costs can be reduced—gathering of medicinal herbs, wild almonds, and firewood—have long been employed. In four years, more than thirty tons of wood have been gathered which, in addition to solving the heating problem, made it possible to assist the production brigades, and also to earn above 200 yuan, which met the various expenses of the school, including equipment.' [1] These words bring to mind the 'country schools' in Cuba. One hesitates to cite such crude experiments as an example, but they give an idea of what a school could do, in less exceptional circumstances, to come closer to the working community.

One should not expect or demand everything from the school, however, even from the secondary school. It does not form such a closed world as it is claimed. To begin with, it admits children who have already had a certain training and learned basic skills

1. This information is taken directly from a study by Léon Vandermeersh on *Educational reform (People's Republic of China)*, published by Unesco in 1972 in the series of documents annexed to the Report of the International Commission on the Development of Education.

and working habits from primary education. Although it is under a duty to prepare those students who leave secondary school to take up employment, it cannot ignore the needs of others who go on to higher education. Both before and after the secondary education stage it is intimately linked with the whole of the education and social system. Nor does it offer the only form of education available to young people of this age group since activities organized around the school and after school and even activities which are not connected with the school in any way, are, in most countries, already assuming an importance which can only increase. The problem of the relationship between education, training and employment cannot, therefore, be completely solved at this level of education alone, any more than the various problems facing education in general. We shall shortly encounter this problem again in a different context.

Chapter three

Problems
and new prospects
in higher education

A considerable amount of work on higher education was carried
out at the international level in 1973 for the second Conference
of Ministers of Education of European Member States [15] and also
in connexion with a study undertaken by OECD [19]. The Conference of Ministers was, of course, concerned with the continent
of Europe as a whole, while the OECD study covered Western
Europe and North America. In both cases, only one part of the
world was directly concerned, although it is this part where most
of the experiments and innovations which are changing the aspect
of higher education originate. Many other countries in other
regions are following these new trends closely, finding in them
a source of ideas or even examples, as is confirmed by the documents emanating from a number of international meetings and by
the reports submitted by various countries to Unesco or the IBE. In
this mass of information, ideas and projects, it is possible to discern
a series of problems and prospects which extend considerably
beyond the confines of the Western world.

WHERE ONE MEETS FAMILIAR PROBLEMS

When the European Ministers of Education held their first conference in November 1967, they concentrated on the problem of access
to higher education. It was, indeed, a time when the number of
students attending university was increasing at a startling rate in
almost every part of Europe. Between 1960 and 1965, the annual
average growth rate in the number of university students for the
continent as a whole was 10 per cent and in one country at least

the figure was higher that 16 per cent. The growth rate of public expenditure on higher education varied from 16 to 28 per cent in sixteen of the twenty-five States studied, whereas their gross national income was increasing at an annual rate of between 9 and 13 per cent. It is easy to appreciate the embarrassment of the public authorities faced with the difficult choice between the principle of free access to higher education, which is the logical application of the right to education but so fraught with danger, and the restriction of admissions by means of selection.

Six years later, when the second Conference of Ministers was held, the problem was no longer so acute. The student tide had abated in the vast majority of European countries and seemed to have levelled off. The question of principle nevertheless remained, and the advocates of restricted and free access clashed again. Most of those in favour of restricted access were the representatives of the socialist States who presented the usual telling arguments, which take the following form. Only over-all planning, covering both economic growth and education, makes it possible to foresee the number of jobs available in each sector of the economy and the desirable number at the higher levels and in each branch of education. In this way, students can be admitted to university so as to satisfy the requirements of society, and can also be distributed among the major branches of instruction. There is no risk of a manpower shortage, nor any danger of unemployment or under-employment. Selection, in any case, is nothing more than the completely objective identification of the most able and most deserving candidates. If selection is not made on admission to higher education, it necessarily occurs either during the course of such education on the basis of examinations or on its completion when degrees are awarded. By restricting access to universities, dropouts, disappointments, bitterness and rebellion are avoided. Of all the countries in the world, the smallest number of dissenting students are to be found in those which practise planning and prior selection. What can be more logical than this argument?

Nevertheless, it failed to convince the sceptics at the Bucharest conference any more than it had, six years earlier, convinced those at the Vienna conference. Governments rejecting the idea of authoritarian distribution and selection are well aware of the dangers of free access. The problem is no longer one of the growing number of students, for most European countries foresee only a small increase in attendance at establishments of higher education. [1] On the other hand, the distribution of students among various branches of study is still a source of concern. The proportion of young graduates taking arts, law, social science or fine arts courses is on the increase almost everywhere, but is declining in the case of science and technological courses. Students are nonetheless given ample warning, and informed how a wrong choice can harm their future career. However, throughout Western Europe, with the exception of Denmark, the tendency of young people to study for an arts or law degree seems as irresistible as the swing away from scientific and technical studies, even in highly industrialized countries such as the Federal Republic of Germany, Switzerland or the Netherlands.

All recent surveys reach the same conclusion that, sooner or later, this imbalance leads to the danger of unemployment or under-employment. [2] The percentage of unemployed social science graduates has doubled in the space of a few years, although admittedly it is not uncommon to find young engineers obliged to take on jobs as ordinary technicians. This would seem to indicate that within one and the same sector, such as technology, the spontaneous distribution of students leaves much to be desired. In addition to this visible unemployment, which can be measured by the discrepancy between supply and demand, there is a kind of latent unemployment. Many arts graduates, fearing that they will not find work quickly, embark upon lengthy research without the slightest assurance that they will be able to make a career as a research worker or university professor.

These phenomena are well known to university authorities and are not, of course, confined to Europe, having been mentioned in the conclusions of the Conference of Ministers of Education of Latin American Countries, held in December 1971. They are also touched upon in the national reports submitted to Unesco by

1. A recent survey undertaken by OECD in sixteen European and three non-European countries (Canada, Japan and the United States) elicited unanimous views on this point [21].

2. See particularly the study published by OECD entitled 'New Relations between post-secondary education and employment' [20].

countries such as Japan, Korea and Mexico. The most accurate information on this subject is, however, available for Europe.

In November 1971, a meeting of specialists was convened by OECD in Grenoble to study the prospects for short-cycle higher education. The imbalance between the various branches of higher education and the disproportion between supply and demand was attributed by them, to some extent at least, to deep-rooted intellectual and social prejudice. In the eyes of young people, traditional universities and the cultural heritage of which they justly claim to be the most illustrious repositories represent 'choice' sectors, whereas technological institutes and subjects are often felt to be second rate. There is, moreover, a hierarchy of careers to match this hierarchy of prestige, the 'choice' sectors leading to top jobs and the others offering less exciting prospects. This led participants in the Grenoble meeting to condemn *de facto* inequality of opportunity [19, p. 311].

Most of the problems found in secondary education are also to be encountered in higher education, and include lack of guidance, inequality of opportunity, abandonment of courses, and an imbalance between teaching, training and employment. This is not surprising. In a country like the United States where the number of college and university students accounts for half of the corresponding age group (i.e. the 20-24-year age group according to international standards), higher education long ago became a mass operation and it is not surprising that it should raise problems for the masses. In Canada, Japan and other countries in the same situation, a similar attitude is already being adopted—as well as in the Soviet Union where the enrolment rate in higher education is 23 per cent. In many Western European countries, on the other hand, where this rate varies between 15 and 22 per cent, one will have to become accustomed to changes of outlook. The time is definitely past when universities trained a privileged élite. Indeed higher education could not very well remain distinct from the rest of the education system, following on, as it does after the mass education now provided at the secondary level. Higher education is at present an integral part of the education system, subject to the influence of the changes which have occurred at lower levels and also, as the culminating point of the system as a whole, to a great extent providing it with a sense of direction.

It cannot be denied that strict planning and authoritarian distribution and selection offer radical solutions for most of these problems, but this approach is associated with a régime found in only a small number of countries. The others have not lost hope of finding more liberal answers and are engaging in more and more research and experiments and, in some cases, even having recourse to expedients.

THE SEARCH FOR NEW SOLUTIONS

It is, in fact, quite correct to speak of expedients when countries such as Finland, the Federal Republic of Germany and Sweden and very recently the Netherlands, while retaining the principle of free access to university, introduced restrictions to limit the number of admissions to certain branches of study, particularly medicine. Authorities which adopt this kind of measure, said to be temporary, have undoubtedly been forced to do so in the face of situations which have become dangerous owing to enormous numbers of students, inadequate accommodation, the danger of lower teaching standards, an imbalance between supply and demand, and the prospect of unemployment. These authorities are not happy about their decisions, however. Restricting the number of students, which is an exceptional measure, is never a satisfactory solution.

Surprise is often expressed at the fact that France continues to maintain its hybrid system under which, for more than a hundred years, universities open to all students with a secondary school leaving certificate have existed side by side with the 'grandes écoles' which turn out the country's top-level men and to which admission is strictly limited. Here, selection exists happily side by side with the democratization of higher education. Yet the situation is no different in the United States. Although any young American with the right qualifications can gain admission to a university or college, not everyone is admitted to the highly-reputed universities such as Harvard, Yale or Princeton. A liberal society based on free competition cannot avoid discrepancies in the quality of education, differences in standing among its university institutions and, consequently, selection for admission to the best of them.

The example of the United Kingdom is even more revealing. British universities have always been free to choose their students and limit their numbers. Although the Government refuses to overcrowd the universities or set up new ones, it recently decided to open up a new avenue leading to higher education by establishing a new type of institution leading to a new type of degree. This led the United Kingdom to establish its famous Open University. It will thus be possible to maintain the number of undergraduates at its present level while enabling 750,000 additional students to obtain higher education between now and 1981. As is well known, the Open University combines correspondence courses, so widely used in the United States and the Soviet Union, with radio and television broadcasts, personal contact with its 40,000 or so students being maintained through various regional centres. The Open University idea, which is similar to the multi-media system, tried out in Quebec for adult education, seems to have won over the Federal German authorities and the Governments of Japan and the Republic of Korea. Although the university of the air is still in the planning stage in the Federal Republic of Germany and Japan, the University Radio and Correspondence College, established as part of the University of Seoul, already had over 12,000 students in 1972 studying public administration, business management, agriculture and education. These new establishments are modelled by and large on the British pattern and seem to have a bright future in store for them, provided the instruction offered can be maintained at the requisite level.[1]

In several other European countries, the aim has been rather to make university admission possible for candidates who have been unable to complete their secondary education and therefore do not possess the necessary qualifications. In Finland, all that is needed is a special decision by the university authorities. In Sweden, a recent measure enables a student to go on to higher education after only two years of secondary education, provided that he passes aptitude tests. French universities hold special

1. Information about the Federal Republic of Germany, the Republic of Korea and Japan comes from the reports submitted by these States to the International Conference on Education. For the Open University in the United Kingdom and other similar institutions, see the book by H. de Saedeleer, *De open universiteit* [45].

entrance examinations, except in the case of medicine, for candidates who do not have a secondary school leaving certificate. In the Soviet Union, students who have not completed their ten-year education may still go on to higher education if they have attended technical establishments for eight years. Elsewhere, already in Yugoslavia and soon in Hungary, actively employed adults are allowed to embark upon higher education corresponding to their professional background.

Although secondary education is still the normal path that leads to higher education in all countries, attempts are at least being made to broaden the basis for admission and to make entrance conditions more flexible, taking into account skills and experience acquired outside school. These changes, which have occurred mainly in the last few years, demonstrate the desire of the authorities to democratize higher education and reconcile the maintenance of a high standard of education with changes in society. The possibilities of hybrid systems are being explored to an increasing extent as offering a middle course between the principle of free access and that of selection.

SHORT-CYCLE EDUCATION

The greatest progress has been made with the introduction of higher education of a shorter duration than that offered by the universities. The twofold aim of this system is to relieve the universities of a number of students who might overcrowd them and gain nothing from being there, and to provide employment opportunities for a steadily growing number of young people. The pattern was set by the United States in the shape of junior colleges which, at the end of secondary education, offer a wide range of courses in the most varied subjects, with the prospect of the student obtaining a valid degree in two years. There were 18 such colleges in 1900 and over 1,000 in 1970. This type of institution has flourished in Canada and, more recently, in Japan. Certain European countries such as Norway and Yugoslavia have, in their turn, opened establishments for short-cycle higher education which very much resemble universities in the range of subjects offered, although their standard is not as high and entrance is easier.

TABLE 2. Short-cycle higher education in seven industrialized countries

Country	1965/66		1972/73	
	Total number of students	Short-cycle higher education[a]	Total number of students	Short-cycle higher education[a]
Fed. Rep. of Germany	—	—	662 232	125 794 (*19.0 %*)
Canada[b]	364 100	63 652 (*18.4 %*)	652 176	168 466 (*25.8 %*)
United States[b]	6 389 872	1 325 970 (*20.8 %*)	9 297 787	2 670 934 (*28.7 %*)
France[b]	458 409	1 644 (*0.4 %*)	737 360	35 422 (*4.8 %*)
Japan	1 182 343	165 291 (*14.0 %*)	2 007 870	376 310 (*18.7 %*)
Poland	339 508	87 644 (*25.8 %*)	429 646	65 372 (*15.2 %*)
Yugoslavia	184 923	68 650 (*37.1 %*)	301 758	91 517 (*30.3 %*)

a. The term 'short-cycle education' refers in fact to the following types of education : Canada : community colleges and other similar institutions ; France : *Instituts universitaires de technologie* ; Federal Republic of Germany : *Fachhochschulen* ; Japan : junior and technical colleges ; Poland : post-secondary vocational schools ; United States : establishments of higher education offering a two-year course ; Yugoslavia : non-university higher education (lasting two years).

b. The figures for Canada are for 1971/72 instead of 1972/73, and those for the United States and France are for 1966/67 instead of 1965/66.

Source : Office of Statistics, Unesco.

Most other European countries have long offered technical education of a higher standard than that available in secondary schools. Since about 1965, however, there has been a vast reform movement which led in France to the establishment of University Institutes of Technology, commonly known as IUT, in Belgium to the introduction of higher technical education, and in the Federal Republic of Germany to the reorganization of the *Fachhochschulen*. The arrangements vary, but the feature that all these establishments have in common is that, within technological fields of varying specialization, they offer short-cycle education lasting two or three years and lead to degrees which are of immediate value in the labour market.

Also about 1965, the United Kingdom opted for a dual system of higher education in which universities exist side by side with a network of non-university colleges for advanced further education. These colleges are not, however, all at the same level, and highest are the polytechnics. The courses they offer are almost as varied as those at universities, but they are shorter, do not aim as high and the degrees awarded do not carry the same weight as traditional university degrees.

Other, even wider horizons for short-cycle higher education have just been opened up by the creation in the United Kingdom of a new kind of establishment of higher education to which several hundred thousands of students are to be admitted and France has introduced the first university cycle at the end of which the general university studies diploma (commonly known as DEUG) is awarded. The aim in both cases is to provide rapid employment opportunities for students unable to take long courses, either for reasons of aptitude or because they cannot afford it.

Although short-cycle education makes it possible to overcome many known difficulties, it must be admitted that it raises certain other serious problems. More even than a long period of education, a short period requires a stable and guaranteed connexion between the training provided and employment prospects. This implies that the degrees it leads to must carry a sufficient weight among employers. If not, there would be grave danger of unemployment and, above all, under-employment. Sooner or later, the future of a form of education unable to guarantee suitable employment for its graduates would be irrevocably compromised. It is therefore of the greatest importance that the public authorities should carefully follow the careers of short-cycle higher education graduates. In this respect, a study carried out by OECD of the French IUT reached reassuring conclusions, as it was found that, from the point of view of both quality and quantity of jobs, the French economy was capable of absorbing many more graduates than these establishments could produce. However, the assurance of immediate employment is not enough to provide an incentive. Young people are much more concerned about their future careers than about the first job they take. As the author of the study quite rightly stated : 'This correlation between career prospects and level at entry is clearly a disincentive for the short-cycle higher education graduate.... Career development must be completely dissociated from the level of entry into that career, and this dissociation must be made known by clear example. This is, of course, a long-term policy, but should be undertaken without delay if we want short-cycle higher education graduates to go straight into active life. Their diploma should be a criterion of fitness only for the first job, because there are no other criteria ; later, a sounder assessment should be made of the worker's aptitudes and his diploma forgotten. [1]

It is by no means certain that the degrees introduced for the first university cycle, or in the United Kingdom for the new establishments offering short-cycle higher education, lead to as many employment opportunities as those of the specialized institutions. Experience alone will make it possible to tell. In any event, and bearing the economic position of various countries in mind, the warning we have quoted remains a salutory one. Whatever form short-cycle higher education takes, it cannot attract large numbers of students unless career prospects appear as favourable as the promise of a first job.

This leads us to a second problem which is even more serious than the first. Teachers from short-cycle higher education attending an OECD symposium in Grenoble complained about the low esteem in which the public and industry held this kind of education in comparison with the prestige they attached to the universities. Teachers in short-cycle education have neither the same qualifications, the same working conditions nor the same pay scales as those in universities. The course is shorter, of course, but also of a lower standard ; no research is done and the students themselves feel they are second-class citizens, whence an inferiority complex. What the colleges offering the short form of education must not do, however, is to try and give themselves university status in order to gain prestige. There are many examples of junior colleges in the

---

1. See the book *Short-cycle higher education*, previously quoted [19], containing the study by Michel-Yves Bernard : 'Problems of employment for graduates of short-cycle higher education and French experience with University Institutes of Technology' (p. 283-311).

United States which have organized supplementary courses and have begun to confer university degrees, claiming the status of traditional universities. In these circumstances, all the advantages of short-cycle education are lost. This is obviously not the way in which to enhance the prestige of short-cycle education. As Professor Burton Clark wrote in his comments about the Grenoble meeting : 'A full parity of esteem will generally not be achievable . . . . Thus the new institutions do not need to chase the rainbow of full equality of status with the universities. What they need in the short run is a level of self-esteem and public legitimacy that allows them to get on with their special work' [19, p. 392]. This is why OECD gave the sub-title 'A search for identity' to its study on short-cycle higher education.

There are thus two sides to the problem. On the one hand, short-cycle higher education has to assert and demonstrate its usefulness and even, so to speak, its quality by doing well what it is responsible for doing in its own field and at its own level. On the other hand, it must not remain immured within its confines like a sealed universe. Students taking the short courses, if they have the ambition and aptitude, should be able to go on to a higher level of education in the universities or the 'grandes écoles', just as those who start work must subsequently have the careers prospects which the quality of their work merits. Whether in employment or in the education system, mobility and promotion are the essential conditions which society has a duty to provide in order to give short-cycle education the chance to prove itself and fulfil its functions.

Advancement in employment is a social matter, which goes far beyond the possibilities of the education system. The structure of the system, of course, varies from one country to another. The simplest solution to avoid compartmentalization and to promote mobility would doubtless be to integrate the short-cycle establishments with the universities. This is the course chosen by France for its IUT and the path which the Federal Republic of Germany has recently decided to follow with regard to its new multi-purpose universities. Integration, of course, does not solve all problems at a stroke and it is surely illogical, not to say absurd, that the IUT should be the only university establishments in France where admission depends on an individual examination of the candidate's files or, in other words, on selection. Many other obstacles remain to be surmounted before total integration is achieved but the law and structures lend themselves to this task. On the other hand, this solution is impossible and unnecessary in the United Kingdom because of the dual higher education system, and even more so in the United States which does not have a national system but a vast mosaic of public or private institutions. The main thing, in any case, is not to look for a single solution. What matters is that regulations and customs should be flexible enough to prevent short-cycle education becoming, to use a word dear to opponents of the established order, a 'ghetto' from which it is no longer possible to escape.[1]

GUIDANCE

When the authorities do not decide for them, how do students choose between long and short-cycle education, between the major branches of study and, within each of these branches, between the subjects offered ? Under a liberal system, guidance assumes vital importance. If the statistics are to be believed, guidance must often be poor, since lack of balance in distribution, failures, students abandoning their courses and examples of unemployment and under-employment are not indications of sound guidance. At the Conference of European Ministers of Education in Bucharest, those who condemned the disadvantages of freedom of choice without adequate guidance were countered by others who said that higher education, even when not completed and even when it did not lead to immediate employment, was never wasted. The knowledge or skills acquired could be useful later in unexpected circumstances and culture absorbed was never lost. It is, of course, quite true that one must not confuse a course of study with the degree it leads to, nor this degree with the recognition of a right to a certain kind of job. In the case of most students, however, these arguments have little chance of being heeded. In a tough society where competition is merciless, how many can afford the

1. See on this topic : Draheim, H. The *Gesamthochschule* : a model of mobility. *Prospects* (Unesco, Paris), vol. III, no. 4, Winter 1973, p. 504-514.

luxury of devoting long years of their youth to acquiring culture for the sake of culture ? Culture is not absorbed or given at one point in time, but acquired through constant effort ; a lifetime is scarcely sufficient. Nobody would dream of denying that the universities are excellent culture centres, but they are surely more than that too.

The problem of guidance clearly remains unsolved, even after the Conference of Ministers. It is obviously no longer a case, as in secondary education, of a process which involves teams of teachers, psychologists and advisers. University students, as adults, have to guide themselves. They can nevertheless be helped by accurate information about careers and labour market prospects, by an open dialogue with their professors and by frequent contact with the working world. All this no doubt occurs to a greater or lesser degree, and universities frequently maintain close contacts with industry, agriculture or commerce. Working exchanges take place between them, and large firms willingly subsidize research which may be useful to them and take an interest in the advanced training of the technicians, engineers or other specialists they need. It must nevertheless be admitted that there is still not enough to facilitate the guidance of students.

The truth is that the effects of specialization in secondary education carry over into higher education. For many students, the die is already cast before they even reach university or establishments offering short courses. The gates which have closed behind them can be opened only with difficulty. It is unusual for a young person who has been directed to the arts side at school to become a scientist or technician at university. Everything militates towards his remaining on the arts side unless he turns to law or possibly the social sciences or economics. This is where lack of balance and poor distribution originate. Successful guidance must begin as early as secondary education.

There are certainly loopholes. Further education between secondary and traditional higher education can give young people time to think and can open up new horizons for them, but this form of education must still remain fairly flexible in order to avoid premature specialization. This was also the aim of the French pre-university course (*propédeutique*) which did not have a long life, and it is still, in part at least, the benefit that France hopes will accrue from the university cycle. Nevertheless, the broad choices have already been made, even at this stage. This is why the French Outline Act on Higher Education, adopted in 1968, placed the principle of interdisciplinarity in the forefront of the reform since it has a bearing both on the organization and the content of education. Interdisciplinarity is based on research experiments and on the introduction of new subjects on which co-operation between specialists with different backgrounds is vital, and has the great advantage of putting an end to traditional compartmentalization. At the same time, although it is a necessity for many research workers, it can also affect the attitude of students in a beneficial way, spare them from premature specialization and, at the administrative level, foster exchanges and changes of course. The new multi-purpose institutions in the Federal Republic of Germany (*Gesamthochschulen*), the subject groups tried out in certain British universities, and the interdisciplinary programmes offered by some universities in the Soviet Union are examples of what could be done in this way.

PARTICIPATION

Whatever is done and whatever success is achieved, it is always the students who, in the last resort, must make their own choice. They must therefore be made to feel responsible for their future and be treated as responsible persons. It will be recalled that 'participation' was the principal claim made by students in the great protest movement which, from 1965 onwards, rocked many universities throughout the world. For these students, to participate was to become responsible partners in the administration of their universities, the organization of their courses and decisions affecting their working conditions. Without perhaps being aware of it, they were giving a modern slant to the old mediaeval concept of universities as communities of teachers and pupils.

It is a fact well worth considering that throughout the world, with the exception of France, the old university structures have withstood the assaults of protest. Nothing has apparently changed in frequently age-old traditions. In most countries, however, students are now represented on the joint bodies which have a say in the running of their establishments. The extent of their representation varies from one country to another and in France, for example, the 1968 Outline Act on Higher Education provides that the proportion of student delegates on councils responsible for educational matters shall be 50 per cent, and 25 or 30 per cent on other councils. Finland is still debating whether professors and students should have equal voting rights. Even if they seem less liberal, provisions of the same kind have been adopted in Austria, Bulgaria, Hungary, Netherlands, Sweden and the United Kingdom. It is perhaps open to discussion whether student participation has achieved all that was expected of it. At a meeting on this topic held in Dubrovnik in 1970, the most sceptical were already saying that, under the guise of participation, the real aim was to take the wind out of the sails of protest, absorb the students into the official system and get their delegates to sanction policies which the students did not wish to support. It also happens, as in France, that many students abstain from elections, but this is a traditional attitude in that country due to indifference rather than to mistrust. Most national reports nevertheless point to the beneficial aspects of participation. Even if its effects are not always conclusive, it constitutes an irreversible trend towards practical forms of democracy.

One cannot, however, close one's eyes to the fact that student participation does not simplify university administration. A modern university, by the number of people—students, teachers and other staff—for which it is responsible, the material and financial resources they employ and the complexity of the problems which have to be solved each day, is akin to the largest of modern industries. Its functional independence, recognized in all countries and under all régimes, squares uneasily with the increasing responsibility assumed by the State for its financing. The administration of an establishment is becoming a specialist affair. This means that, like other undertakings of similar size, there is a danger of universities becoming like companies—faceless and without personal relationships among partners. This, at the same time, would bring to nought all attempts at democratization, all educational innovations and all the benefits of participation. It is awareness of this danger which leads certain students to compare themselves to workers in industry, and their associations to trade unions. This is no doubt an erroneous comparison although it is, to a large extent, understandable. If this tendency were to be followed, participation would become a kind of permanent confrontation between employers and employees, and nothing of the university community would be left. We have not yet reached that stage but the danger is a real one, and we must be aware of it. Of all the problems confronting higher education, the problem of university administration is certainly not the least.

THE STUDY AND EXAMINATION SYSTEM

The most frequent and most justified criticism made of the university system as it existed until recently in many European countries was that there was no contact between students and teachers. Crowded universities are hardly the right place to form personal relationships and professors did not know, or barely knew, the names of their students. The students, for their part, left to themselves, felt that they were lost in the crowd. End-of-year examinations, frequently anonymous in order to be fair, left a great deal to luck and encouraged last-minute cramming, that intense and hasty study during the weeks prior to the examination date. All these grievances are so well known that there is no point in dwelling on them.

To believe that everything has changed for the better since the great protest would be to harbour illusions. It must nevertheless be admitted that the system of study has changed considerably. Those celebrated lectures, given to an anonymous and impassive crowd, have often been replaced by work in small groups. Students are split into teams and supervised by teachers who know them, so that they receive more effective guidance. The system of continuous assessment has often taken the place of end-of-year examinations. All over Europe, these changes inevitably led to a rapid increase in the number of teachers, professors or assistants; between 1965 and 1970, the annual growth rate was 6 to 7 per cent in Europe and 7 to 8 per cent in North America. This trend is, in any case, world-wide, since in other parts of the world growth rates are similar or even higher (10 per cent in Latin America and over 11 per cent in Africa and the Arab States). However, as the number of students rose in similar proportions during the same period, the problem of the staff/student ratio in higher education is far from being solved.

Although this new system of study and examinations has considerable advantages, it also has its drawbacks. It is difficult to see how it could be applied to part-time students who are prevented by their employment from attending courses, practical or laboratory work with any great regularity. Although the number of such students is not accurately known at present, it will no doubt increase rapidly. It is true that evening classes and holiday courses are organized for them, and that in some university colleges, the continuous year system is being adopted. Yet it is easy to imagine what difficulties this causes, as ingrained habits, the timetables of professors and financial obstacles have to be contended with. University organization and strictly limited budgets do not lend themselves very readily to this kind of innovation. Even in the case of full-time students, it is doubtful whether it is in their best interests to try too hard to provide staff and supervision for them, impose unduly strict attendance requirements and assess them unceasingly. It is surely right that these proud young people, who justly demand to be considered as responsible partners, should assume their due share of responsibility for the organization of their work, for their success and even for their failure. This is the only way in which they will maintain that spirit of initiative and independence which is in the best student tradition.

On the other hand, extension of the 'value units' system, long known in the United States by the name of credits, can be nothing but beneficial. Under this system, a student, whether young or adult, is credited with integrated units of knowledge and these he can save up and use when the right time comes in order to obtain the appropriate university diplomas. A system as flexible as this fosters mobility, new lines of activity and that alternation between study and work which is so desirable. It provides conditions for genuine progress in culture, work and society alike. The day is perhaps not so distant when our old universities, following the example of the community colleges in America, will credit their students with the qualities they have shown in practical work side by side with the knowledge they have acquired in their studies.

THE FUNCTION OF HIGHER EDUCATION

At the conclusion of their discussions, the European Ministers of Education in Bucharest attempted to define the essential functions of higher education in a joint formula. This was how it ran [5c, p. 7] :

'As to the ultimate purpose of higher education, many delegations stressed that it had in recent years emerged as being twofold : firstly, to train highly-qualified specialists to meet the requirements of the economy and of society ; secondly, to extend to an ever greater number of young people and adults the benefit of a high standard of education whilst at the same time providing them with cultural, moral and civic training, thus enabling them to develop fully as individuals and members of society and helping to strengthen their moral fibre. Most speakers emphasized the need, in order to achieve that end, to maintain the unity of teaching and research, and also to combine theoretical and practical training. Such practical training should enable students to familiarize themselves with research work and with production processes. Higher education would thus contribute to social progress and to the promotion of democracy within society.'

It cannot be expected that an official text of this kind, resulting from a compromise between frequently opposing views, will shed much new light on the subject. Here, however, one's attention is caught by at least two ideas, the first of which is the importance attached to research. Research has always been recognized as one of the essential functions of higher education. In Soviet universities, the time devoted by a professor to scientific work is even included among his functions. This measure is in the interest not only of the professor but also, and mainly, his students since learning how to conduct research is considered an integral part of their practical training. It is not specified at what level of study this learning should begin, whether at the stage of the masters' degree, as in the second cycle in French universities, or at the third stage when studying for a doctorate, or again, as in the Italian Government's plans, at an even higher level which calls for the establishment of a new research doctorate. It is nevertheless possible to envisage students being introduced to research in a more modest form from the very start of their university course. This opens up a vast prospects for bold reforms.

The second noteworthy feature of this passage is its reference to adults. Students in higher education have, of course, reached adult age, but this is obviously not what the European Ministers had in mind. The adults they were considering were men and women already employed who, by their age, maturity and working experience, and also because of gaps in their previous education, were no longer young people like the majority of students. Many establishments of higher education, either within universities or independently of them, have long organized correspondence, radio or television courses for adults. The European Ministers of Education nevertheless wished to assert that, in their view, higher education was henceforth to recognize them all, young and adult, as its own and admit them all on an equal footing. This is the sign of a fundamental change. A considerable distance can still separate a declaration of principle from practical reality. A step has nevertheless been taken and the movement which has been initiated here also seems irreversible.

One of the foreseeable consequences of this change of attitude will be the more rapid organization of a genuine lifelong education. On this point, there was complete agreement between the conclusions reached by the ministers and those in the OECD study on short-cycle higher education. Even if reformed, diversified and made widely available to young people and adults, higher education will never manage to cope with all those who deserve admission. The whole of life ought to offer men and women a final opportunity for education. As it is appropriate to let the Ministers responsible have their say, we shall take one last quotation from the Final Report of the Bucharest Conference [6c, p. 14] :

'It was the general opinion of the Commission that the fundamental importance of lifelong education lay in the fact that it helped to facilitate, at one and the same time, the participation of all age-groups in all types and levels of education, the professional and social advancement and cultural development of those in employment, and the constant updating of knowledge that scientific and technological progress demanded.'

In our discussion of secondary education, our attention was focused primarily on the difficulties of the Third World, but in examining the new prospects for higher education, we considered certain developed countries. This obviously does not mean that other countries never question the future of their universities or that nothing worthy of note is happening there. Unlike primary and secondary education, however, which have to adapt to the conditions specific to each region or country, university education throughout the world to a large extent has the same objectives and problems because of the universal nature of knowledge and research. While it is therefore legitimate to think in terms of a school which is specifically African, it is difficult to conceive of a university which would deliberately turn its back on its universal calling. This is why, by mentioning the experiments carried out in a limited number of countries, we do not feel that we have neglected the interests of the others. In this respect, Europe and North America continue to play the necessary role of trail blazers for the benefit of all.

Chapter four

A stage in adult education

The conference held in Tokyo from 25 July to 7 August 1972 was the third to be organized by Unesco on adult education; the first had taken place at Elsinore, Denmark, in the spring of 1949 and the second in Montreal during the summer of 1960. A large gathering of this kind, bringing together delegations designated by Governments, does not have the same character or the same objectives as an educational congress. It offers no opportunity for propounding personal theories or for doing pioneer work, and a specialist may return home with the impression of having learnt nothing really new. On the other hand, what it does offer is a unique opportunity for measuring the distance travelled at the international level, for evaluating the progress achieved and the difficulties that remain to be overcome, and for identifying the major trends emerging in various countries. Like its predecessors, the Tokyo Conference was a reflexion of contemporary reality.

FROM ELSINORE TO TOKYO VIA MONTREAL

At Elsinore, 25 States were represented; at Montreal there were 51, and in Tokyo, 87. This increase is explained by the growing number of Unesco's Member States. Since, in 1949, the Soviet Union still held aloof from the Organization, other European socialist countries did not reply to the invitation. What has, since then, been termed the Third World was represented by only five delegations—three from Asia, one from Latin America and one from Africa. Western Europe and North America predominated,

and what was mainly heard was the voice of countries where adult
education had already become firmly entrenched, such as the
Scandinavian States, the United Kingdom, Canada or the United
States. Very little was said about the illiteracy problem, which was
then only of secondary importance to such highly-developed countries. Because, for practical reasons, vocational training was
excluded from the discussions, attention was focused on cultural
action directed towards the development of culture for the people
at large, in order to end the traditional 'opposition between the
so-called masses and the so-called élite'. To round off this descrip-
tion of the theme of the Elsinore discussions, it may be pointed out
that the conference report, without ignoring the role of the State
and local authorities, highlighted the efforts of voluntary organizations, private or denominational associations, professional and
trade union bodies, and co-operative movements.

Eleven years later, at the Montreal meeting, there had been a
considerable evolution in ideas. The achievement of independence
by a large number of peoples and their mass entry onto the international scene, the prodigious progress of technology, and the
empire that television had already carved out for itself, reflected
a variety of situations and offered a host of new prospects. The
central theme selected for the second Conference was, therefore,
'Adult education in a changing world'. The most striking feature
of the final report of the Montreal Conference is the forceful
assertion of the principle that '... people everywhere should come
to accept adult education as normal, and that governments should
treat it as a necessary part of the educational provision of every
country'. Integration, then, is the first demand, but we should also
note the appeal addressed to governments. Although at Montreal,
as at Elsinore, there was still vigorous support for the role of
private organizations and for the cause of liberty or diversity, other
delegations were not hard put to reply that the immensity of needs,
like the massive use of modern technology, had created a new
situation for which the authorities should assume responsibility.
Another significant fact was that the eradication of illiteracy was
to head the list of any order of priorities drawn up. Certain resolutions urged more active participation by the schools and the
teaching profession in adult education, the full use of school premises and facilities, and wider involvement of the universities.

With regard to adult educators, the Montreal report points out that they have the feeling of exercising a profession which should be provided with a statutory basis. As a crowning touch, the Conference called for extensive aid to the developing countries. [1]

In inviting Member States to the Tokyo meeting, the General Conference of Unesco requested them to make thorough preparations for it. This appeal did not go unheeded, as is proved by the ninety-seven national reports which were submitted by the participating States and which constitute an inexhaustible source of information. [2] The agenda of the Conference, as much as the working documents, gives an idea of the scope of the proceedings: main trends in adult education during the last ten years ; role and place of adult education in integrated education systems within the context of lifelong education ; planning, administration and financing problems ; new methods and techniques ; training of personnel ; development of adult education through international co-operation. None of the major issues faced by educators, the competent organizations or the State was excluded from the Tokyo discussions and although, as at all large international gatherings, there was insufficient time to go into as much detail as desirable, the final report constitutes a compendium of thinking, experience and suggestions of incomparable importance. Anyone reading it is filled with the conviction that the Tokyo meeting was a milestone in the long course of adult education [3].

AN UNBOUNDED DOMAIN

If we confine ourselves to the field of education, whether school or university, the age of pupils and students suggests certain limits, established by custom, and international statistics can provide relatively accurate figures as regards numbers. But when we venture into the domain of adult education, what criterion can be

1. The reports published by Unesco on the Elsinore and Montreal Conferences can be consulted, as well as the work by Arnold S.M. Hely [10].

2. These reports have been reproduced on microfiches as part of the Unesco : IBE SIRE series, in Geneva. Several have also been published in the quarterly review *Convergence*, published in Toronto (Canada), in English, Spanish, French and Russian.

used to define its boundaries ? By what means do we identify a person as belonging to the adult category ? In a highly developed country we can, at a pinch, fall back on the length of the compulsory schooling period or the age group corresponding to the average of the young people concerned. This is how, as we have already seen, universities distinguish adults from ordinary students. But for the developing countries the age criterion is of no practical value : adolescents and even children who have never attended school—like the hundreds of millions of illiterates throughout the world—come within the province of adult education. It is true that, in order to evaluate the extent of illiteracy, certain conventions have had to be adopted in international statistics, such as recognition of every illiterate of at least 15 years of age as an adult. But how can an educator make use of such a convention ? In education, each youngster represents an individual case. And since at the other end of the scale there is no limit other than that of the span of human life, education must indeed adjust itself to the dimensions of the world population. As regards age, adult education knows no limit.

Neither is there anything compulsory about it ; everything depends on the personal inclination of the adult. We can quite well visualize adult education as something without any structure or institution, for it is sufficient to take advantage of the opportunities and facilities provided by society. In this respect, the lavishness of modern consumer societies is without precedent, both in terms of the annual production of books and periodicals, encyclopaedias, films, reproductions of works of art and radio or television broadcasts ; as well as in terms of the countless numbers of concerts, exhibitions, theatre or cinema shows, libraries or museums. An adult who feels the need to educate himself or improve his mind, if fortunate enough to live in a highly developed society, will have only too much to choose from. Our epoch is the golden age for the self-learner. The Tokyo Conference took care, furthermore, to enter the extension of the self-learning process on the credit side of the adult education ledger.

The pursuit of one's education alone requires a great deal of will-power, powerful incentives and, most important of all, unusual perseverance. Hence the value of outside assistance, i.e. a community organization. Here again the field is limitless. From evening and correspondence courses to the people's universities of the Soviet Union and the workers' universities in Yugoslavia, from the modest 'polytechnical villages' in Kenya to the 'universities without walls' of New York and Ohio, from the major co-operative undertakings in Belgium, Switzerland or Canada to the programmes of the *Conservatoire français des arts et métiers*, from the multimedia experiments in Quebec to the Open University in the United Kingdom, from literacy campaigns to the impressive Indian project for the use of a satellite, and from the university of the air in Japan to refresher training courses in industry : all man's imagination and magnanimity, like the constraints of the modern economy, combine to produce an unending stream of new institutions.

Certain figures speak for themselves : in Canada, close on 750,000 persons attended courses for adults given by secondary education teachers in 1971, and such was the diversity of the subjects offered that a Toronto library had the excellent idea of setting up an automated information system for the public [16]. During the same year, Sweden was catering to over 2 million persons, or almost half the country's population. When numbers of this magnitude are involved, the efforts of private organizations are no longer sufficient ; all available resources must be mobilized, and all the organizing potential of the local authorities, or even of the State is required. Adult education, regardless how it is organized, becomes a genuine public service, but one based on the voluntary enrolment of the individual and on active participation.

A domain with unlimited inherent possibilities and seeking expression in an infinite variety of ways—this, at first sight, is the main feature of adult education at the present time.

THE FUNCTIONS OF ADULT EDUCATION

Reducing this diversity of aims and means to a single definition of adult education is not an easy task. Like so many others before it, the Tokyo Conference was not completely successful in its attempt. We prefer this passage from the report of the International Commission on the Development of Education [9, p. 205] which has the great merit of clarity and simplicity :

'There are many possible definitions of adult education. For a very large number of adults in the world today, it is a *substitute* for the basic education they missed. For the many individuals who received only a very incomplete education, it is the *complement* to elementary or professional education. For those whom it helps respond to new demands which their environment makes on them, it is the *prolongation* of education. It offers *further education* to those who have already received high-level training. And it is a means of *individual development* for everybody. One or other of these aspects may be more important in one country than in another, but they all have their validity.' [The author's italics.]
We shall therefore adopt this definition, and see whether it is borne out by the facts.

The substitute function : making adults literate

For those who have never had the chance to go to school and are, therefore, illiterate, adult education is really the only possible substitute for the education they did not receive. Ever since Unesco's establishment, authoritative voices have been denouncing the scandal and danger represented by the world's untold masses of illiterates—a scandal from the standpoint of justice and human rights and a danger from the standpoint of international understanding and chances of a lasting peace. In the absence of statistics, the least pessimistic estimates of the total number of illiterates at that time gave the figure as half of the world's population. One of Unesco's initial acts was therefore to embark on a world campaign for universal literacy. Basic education, devised for illiterates, was not confined to teaching people to read and write, but was also aimed at raising standards of living through more efficient agricultural or handicraft techniques and, by fostering a civic sense, at ensuring more active participation in the life of the community. It was the intention, from the very beginning, to help countries in which illiteracy was rampant, in other words practically the whole of Africa, Latin America and Asia, to develop methods and train personnel ; hence the national or regional training and educational research centres which have been set up with international assistance. In order to ensure that those who had become literate

did not lose the reading habit and their taste for books, the production and circulation of various language versions of suitable
literature was also encouraged. The world campaign for universal
literacy, welcomed so enthusiastically, has progressed over a period
of some fifteen years, although not without its ups and downs.

Shortly after 1960 it was perforce recognized that the targets
which had been rather hastily established would not be attained.
Statistics recorded but slow progress, and the initial enthusiasm
waned. It was time to review the facts of the problem more
realistically. This was the situation when, in 1965, Unesco
convened a World Congress of Ministers of Education at Tehran to
consider in general what action should be taken to deal with illiteracy, and from the Tehran recommendations, themselves based
on certain experiments in Iran, emerged the new concept of 'functional literacy'. The main weaknesses of the world campaign were
due to its vast scale and failure to differentiate, as well as to the
absence of any direct relationship between literacy and the
economic development of the countries concerned. If, on the other
hand, attention is focused on the development plan of a certain
country and, within that country, on social and economic conditions in a specific region, and if fairly homogeneous groups of
illiterate workers are identified, programmes can be formulated
that are geared specifically to the needs of these groups, to regional
development needs and to those of the nation as a whole. Unlike
the mass literacy campaign, which is based on relatively uniform
and inevitably preconceived methods, functional literacy is, therefore, selective ; it is directed first and foremost at vocational training, which it uses as a point of departure to promote, just like any
other form of education, the development of the personality.

Functional literacy has given new impetus to the campaign
for universal literacy. During 1973, an experimental programme,
supported by international assistance, was being implemented in
sixteen African, Latin American and Asian countries : Afghanistan,
Algeria, Ecuador, Ethiopia, Guinea, India, Iran, Kenya, Madagascar,
Mali, Niger, Sudan, Syrian Arab Republic, United Republic of
Tanzania, Venezuela and Zambia. In addition, several other countries received aid during the same year to enable them to prepare
or apply programmes of the same kind [5, p. 59-68].

What are the results that have been achieved by all these

Diagram 1. World adult population and illiteracy rate

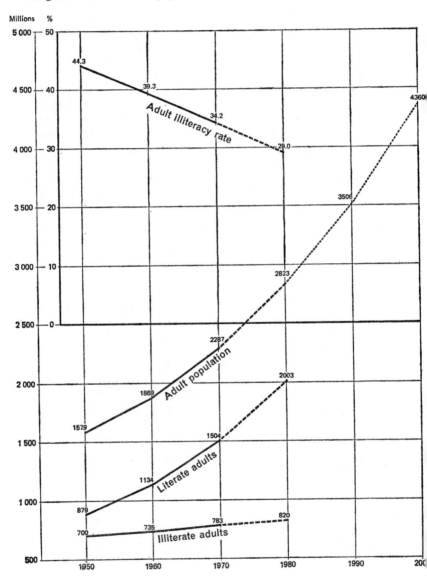

Source: Office of Statistics, Unesco.

efforts of States and international organizations, to eliminate illiteracy ? Around 1950, the percentage of illiterates was estimated at 44.3 per cent of the world adult population ; in 1960 this figure dropped to 39.3 per cent and, in 1970, to 34.2 per cent. Although slow, the progress made is nevertheless appreciable. However, as the world's adult population increased by almost 700 million during the same period, there were 83 million more adult illiterates in 1970 than in 1950. As regards future trends, it is estimated, after making allowance for population growth, that the illiteracy rate will be 29 per cent in 1980 and only 15 per cent by the year 2000. The optimists therefore conclude that, towards the end of the second decade of the twenty-first century, illiteracy will have been stamped out. The pessimists are more conscious of the fact that there are still 783 million illiterates in the world. The whole problem is a function of these two figures and these two dates (see Diagram 1).

The most disturbing aspect is the pattern of illiteracy in the various regions of the world. About 1970, when the proportion of adult illiterates was 34.2 per cent for the world as a whole, North America accounted for only 1.5 per cent and Europe for 3.6 per cent, whereas the proportion was 73.7 per cent in Africa, 73 per cent in the Arab countries, 46.8 per cent in Asia and 23.6 per cent in Latin America. What is striking is not so much the figures themselves as the staggering inequality they reflect. Another distressing feature is the imbalance between men and women, as men account for 63.4 per cent and women for 83.7 per cent of the over-all figure of 73.7 per cent for African illiterates. The same disproportion exists in the Arab countries, whose 60.5 per cent of men and 85.7 per cent of women are illiterate.

Leaving aside the question of future prospects, how is it that, after so much effort and sacrifice to educate children and make adults literate, present results are still so disappointing ? Having exhausted all the usual arguments, such as the cumbersome nature of the educational process, opposition based on prejudice, and the lack of resources—we are forced to face squarely up to the problem. The eradication of illiteracy is not an unreasonable undertaking for those prepared to tackle the problem on a large scale. The Soviet Union did so some time ago and, since then, China and Algeria have embarked on the same course ; Cuba's efforts have been crowned with success. According to reliable witnesses [38], it took the Cubans only a few months to do away illiteracy in 1961. An unprecedented national campaign was launched to mobilize over 120,000 volunteers who, together with 105,000 pupils temporarily released from their schools and 20,000 workers, acted as voluntary teachers in the service of the cause. Before the year was out the campaign was officially declared to be over ; more than 700,000 adults had learned to read and write, and the proportion of illiterates had dropped from 23 to less than 4 per cent.

We may disagree with these methods on the grounds that feats of this kind are possible only in exceptional circumstances. Nevertheless, many governments, facing the difficult choice between the rapid eradication of illiteracy by means of crash programmes or its gradual elimination through the education of children, opt for the latter solution. They are entirely within their rights. Such governments have certainly not turned their backs on the education of their adult population and apply functional literacy programmes conscientiously, but it is to the school that they accord priority. Their first thoughts are for the young, because they represent the future ; adults can wait. This much is clear from the importance that the reports of regional conferences of ministers of education attach to primary, secondary or higher education in comparison with adult education. As long as this situation continues, the existence of large numbers of illiterates, particularly among women, in so many Third World countries, and even in those which are not the poorest, will not be surprising.

A complement to education

Although international statistics on illiteracy are available, none give even an approximate idea of the number of children who drop out of school each year, well before the normal completion of their studies. But judging from the periodical reports received from the developing countries, educational wastage caused by drop-outs must reach terrifying proportions. Education is like a column on the march which abandons a host of footsore stragglers at the roadside. What becomes of these victims of a seemingly incurable malady ? They are not illiterates, for they have been taught to read and write, but on the labour market they scarcely

TABLE 3. Illiteracy and literacy classes in sixteen countries, by region

Country	Year	Illiteracy at 15 years and over (last census)		Participation in literacy classes 1972/73		Population 15 years and over, 1972 (000)
		Number of illiterates	% of illiteracy	Functional	Other	
Algeria	1971	4 656 715	73.6	126 534	–	7 906
Gabon	1960/61	271 629	87.6	150	89	328
Libyan Arab Republic	1964	664 248	78.3	33 137	–	1 105
Niger	1960	1 493 520	99.1	1 923	7 253	2 172
Somalia	–	–	–	2 000	580 500	1 588
Bolivia	1950	1 109 385	67.9	26 097	–	2 800
Chile	1970	629 440	11.9	882	–	6 271
Cuba	1953	820 337	22.1	86 169	27 024	5 792
Dominican Rep.	1970	601 210	31.5	1 158	9 266	2 420
Ecuador	1962	799 535	32.5	62 183	–	3 459
Venezuela	1971	1 007 900	17.6	4 456	12 477	6 333
Indonesia	1971	32 498 850[a]	40.4[a]	639 255	725 997	71 012
Iran	1966	10 368 000	77.0	159 408	113 054	16 431
Iraq	1957	2 979 368	85.5	111 416	–	5 528
Laos	–	–	–	1 781	–	1 810
Singapore	1970	394 543	31.1	3 768	21 719	1 345

a: 10 years and over.

Source: Office of Statistics, Unesco, based on official replies to questionnaire STE/Q/731.

rate any higher. Mostly of peasant origin, they go back to the land or to a rural craft, without any other training than what they pick up from their family. In terms of age, they are children or possibly adolescents, but as the school can do nothing further for them, only adult education is able to offer them a second chance.

A study recently undertaken for the United Nations Children's Fund [26] identified more than 150 informal agricultural training programmes being implemented in 45 countries in the Third World : 13 in Latin America, 8 in Asia, 4 in the Middle East and 20 in Africa. While refraining from drawing conclusions about experiments of such diversity, their nature can be illustrated by reference to the project for the education of adolescents in one of the underprivileged states in Brazil, Pernambuco, the project in Eastern Java, in Indonesia, for young people of under 20, the rural development centres set up in Mali by the pioneer movement, the agricultural education plan in Upper Volta or, again, the 'second chance' programme introduced in Mali. The authors of this study have not sought to gloss over the weaknesses of these experiments, which they term 'out-of-class' programmes, but which could be called more accurately 'nonformal' activities, for they are all organized outside the formal system. Decided upon in haste and lacking sufficient preparation, almost always fragmentary, short of supervisory staff, they would stand to gain by being co-ordinated at the national level or associated with a more systematic project. But even with these shortcomings, they are already yielding most gratifying results.

Another survey [27], conducted this time on the initiative of the World Bank, under the same guidance but in 15 other countries in Africa, Latin America and Asia, [1] has resulted in a more searching analysis of types, conditions, costs and financing methods of informal education for young agricultural workers. The possibilities opened up by these two studies are so vast and the initial results so encouraging that informal education might well be the answer in agriculture, which is of such vital importance to the developing countries.

1. Colombia, Mexico ; Ethiopia, Kenya, Malawi, Nigeria, Senegal, Sudan, United Republic of Tanzania ; Afghanistan, Bangladesh, Republic of Korea, India, Philippines, Thailand.

It has already proved to be a useful complement to education. If we can maintain its diversity and its invaluable flexibility, guard against the temptation to build it up into a system, with all the rigidity and formalism that this would imply, it might even offer the rural population of the Third World countries a valid alternative to the school.

A prolongation of education

We come here to the most familiar function of adult education, the most classic (if this term does not sound too odd in this domain) and the one that has the most firmly established institutions. It is here that it all began, with the evening classes and people's universities of the last century. The desire to offer adults the means of extending the education they acquired in their youth has, for a long time, met a twofold need, by satisfying the thirst for knowledge and culture, shared by such a large number of persons, and by giving workers at all levels the chance of professional advancement. Changes in the modern economy have more recently added a third need, that of retraining, when the need arises, for a new job. It is true that these needs are particularly marked and more often satisfied in the developed countries. For this reason the Elsinore Conference, with its very limited composition, focused most of its attention on this problem. But the developing peoples had more urgent concerns, and therefore the Montreal Conference, its ear more attuned to the voice of the Third World, assigned high priority to the eradication of illiteracy. In Tokyo an effort was made to maintain a balance between the problems of the underprivileged nations and those of the highly industrialized countries. Long experience proves how difficult it is for a world gathering to arrive at a synthesis of an extremely diverse range of aspirations. The task of the Tokyo Conference was, in this respect, particularly arduous, but it has to be recognized that the praiseworthy concern for universality reflected in its final report did not always succeed in concealing an implicit deference to the forms of adult education that responded more particularly to the needs of the most developed societies. This can be sensed in certain statements of principle, the importance attached to questions of organization or financing, in the search for a balance between the public authorities and

trade union or co-operative movements, in short, in the various
kinds of problems which arise mainly when adult education is
the prolongation of instruction that is already firmly established.

Further education

This type of education implies in-service training courses. Generated by the demands of science and technology in their industrial
applications, it was not long before the need for refresher training
came to be felt in all the professions—medicine and public administration alike, teaching as well as business management, agriculture and trade ; not even the clergy has remained unaffected.
This need to bring professional knowledge and skills up to date,
even if expressed more forcefully in the highly technically developed societies, is too widely recognized for the Tokyo Conference to
have deemed it useful to dwell on it. We observe, however, within
the same context, its interest in parent education, this other form
of refresher training, the development of which seemed necessary
for the advancement of democratic education.

A *means of individual development*

After listing the various objectives of adult education, the report
of the Tokyo Conferences reaches the following one, which supplements and covers the others : 'It was an instrument whereby the
whole man, including man at work and man at play, man in his
civic, family and cultural roles, could achieve fulfilment .... Adult
education and cultural development were two elements of a single,
overall process, and it was essential to integrate the two.' [3c,
p. 21-22.] [1] It is indeed high time to put an end to a misunderstanding that has persisted too long. There is often confusion, or
pretended confusion, between adult education and continuing education. The 1971 French Law which recognizes every worker's right
to continuing training is a bold and liberal piece of legislation,
and marks a decisive step forward. But it is confined to in-service
professional training and fails to mention its other aspects and the
cultural development which the Tokyo Conference rightly asserted

1. Reference may also be made to the article on this subject by Anna
Lorenzetto, 'The cultural dimension of adult education' [40].

could not be dissociated from adult education. Admittedly, every-thing cannot be done at once and no doubt the French Government, like Parliament, had good reason for not aiming higher at that time. We must not, however, forget the long road that remains to be travelled before the goal is reached.

All education has as its supreme aim the development of the personality—of the child, the adolescent, the adult. But the task is the most difficult in the case of adults because, much more than children or adolescents, they are subject to the constraints of society, and above all professional and financial constraints. The Tokyo Conference used forceful language in alluding to the emanci-pating power of adult education or, to use a fashionable term, its ability to combat alienation. Even the final report describes it in an unusual way as an instrument of conscientization. This immediately calls to mind Paulo Freire, not only for his well-known theories but also for his memorable literacy experiments in Brazil and Chile. This word 'conscientization', transcribed directly from the Portuguese, means both an awareness of reality, with all its social, political and economic constraints and contra-dictions, as well as the starting point for a struggle against oppres-sive reality. For Paulo Freire, adult literacy is a 'pedagogy of the oppressed' and education in general is the exercise of freedom [29, 30]. Through its association with this idea, albeit a discreet refer-ence, the Tokyo Conference managed to give expression to all the manifold aspects of adult education.

PROBLEMS OF ORGANIZATION

It was in connexion with problems of organization, planning and financing that the Tokyo Conference carried out its most exhaustive analysis and made its most useful contribution [3c, p. 22-26]. The world of adult education, as it appears in the light of the final report, is one of diversity. Its structures and practices vary not only from one country to another, reflecting differences in political systems, ideological trends and national legislation, but even within the same country, for divergent views divide educators whose thinking has been moulded by their experience or philosophy. This we knew before the Tokyo meeting which, however, provided us with striking confirmation.

The new element that emerges from the account of its proceedings is the constant effort to overcome these differences in
circumstances and these divergent opinions, and to identify a
number of principles that will be acceptable to a very large
majority. There is always a danger of treating the collective
deliberations of a large international gathering such as this one in
the same way as individual thinking. The approach is not comparable, the thought process does not follow the same course. However, in reading the final report, we cannot fail to detect signs of
dialectical tension between diametrically opposed viewpoints
although, at the same time, we can discern the outline of a synthesis ; the two viewpoints which are constantly brought into
opposition are, first, the need for integration and, second, the desire
to preserve the original identity of adult education. As for the
synthesis, surely it was suggested beforehand in the general theme
chosen for the Conference : 'Adult education within the context
of lifelong education' ?

The need for integration had already been felt by the Montreal
Conference, but at Tokyo it was asserted much more forcefully
and specifically. In the initial stage, it is simply a matter of the
co-ordination, within the national framework, of public or private
activities, which are steadily expanding, as is the number of people
to whom they cater and the technical or financial resources that
they use. However valuable diversity may be, it must not result
in incoherence, waste or futility. This necessary co-ordination can
be achieved either under the authority of a ministry, in the case of
a country with firmly rooted institutions, or within a national
council, as is done in the English-speaking countries. But the
decision, as regards one solution or another, is up to the State.
Extremely strong objections are immediately raised : nothing is
more detrimental to adult education than excessive centralization.
Since this has to be achieved by the State—which alone has the
power to take the final decision to ensure the efficient planning
of desirable developments and to make available the immense
financial and material resources that are required—then the State
should delegate at least a considerable part of its functions to
regional or local administrative authorities, since they are in closer
touch with the actual situation and more qualified to evaluate the
specific needs of the population. Whatever the country to which

they belong, adult educators are aggressive advocates of decentralization.

The authorities must also take care not to disregard the place
and role of private initiative. As the Tokyo report constantly
reminds us, 'the non-governmental organizations, especially the
trade unions, had a long and important tradition which, in many
cases, antedated action by governments'. Is the political, philosophical or religious diversity of these organizations not the best
guarantee of the 'freedom of expression of the many and varied'
experiments, both for the forces of opposition and for the minorities ? The Conference was unable to opt for a type of organization
that it realized would be unacceptable to certain countries ; it did,
however, suggest more flexible models in which the State would
confine itself to formulating outline laws or establishing joint
management, bringing together its own representatives, those of
regional and local authorities and of the voluntary organizations as
a whole. As may be seen from these examples, selected from
among countless others, the relationship between the State and
private initiative was the focal point of the Tokyo discussions.

But it is in the second stage of integration that problems
assume their most serious aspect. Conscious of the steadily growing
importance of their function, adult educators no longer wish to be
the 'poor relations'. They demand that the rights and needs of the
adult be recognized just like those of the child or adolescent. Adult
education must henceforth become an integral part of every
national education project. Of all the chapters in the final report
of the Tokyo Conference, the most vibrant is unquestionably the
one dealing with 'adult education and its relationship with formal
and school education', containing as it does cutting references to
'educational privileges denied to the masses', the 'increasingly
anomalous and paralysing perpetuation of an education system
which alone swallowed up ... a third of the country's budget' or,
again, to the inculcation by the school of 'modes of thought and
"intellectual" behaviour patterns which were ill-suited to development requirements...'. All the forces of dissent as regards the
school system seem to have been unleashed at Tokyo, to the point
that certain delegations—and it is not difficult to guess which they
were—deemed it necessary to reply 'stoutly and clearly', as the
report states, that there was no crisis in their schools nor did their

'young people, teachers and parents ... challenge the existing education system'. The report notes further that representatives of
several developing countries were 'disconcerted by such attacks
on the school system' [3c, p. 22-23].

It is not that the vast majority of adult educators refuse to
co-operate with the school ; they would, on the contrary, like to
receive more support from its teachers and have greater access
to school premises and facilities ; they would like the universities to
open their doors wider to adults. All forms of co-operation were
referred to in Tokyo. But adult educators realize that their teaching
practices are more diversified and daring than those of the school,
and also geared more closely to development requirements. They
are aware that a comparison between what they give and what
they receive in many cases tips the scales in their favour. Adult
education must not lose its identity in the integration which they
regard as necessary.

THE PRINCIPLE OF LIFELONG EDUCATION

Since adult education cannot and does not want to become integrated into the education system, integration can be achieved only
as part of an over-all education project which will transcend both
systems. The Tokyo discussions took place 'within the context of
lifelong education'. An evocative idea, but one that demands interpretation. Lifelong education might well serve as a context, but
only from the point of view of concepts and not of facts, for
nowhere has lifelong education become a reality. Certain recent
reforms, as in Japan or Peru, have admittedly chosen it as their
objective ; others refer to it as a yardstick. It opens up immense
prospects, arouses great expectations and has already provided
material for a large number of works, as is demonstrated by one
international bibliography [14] listing as it did in 1972 almost
300 titles of books or articles in which lifelong education is
expressly mentioned. But it must also be recognized that there is
considerable confusion about the meaning of this term.

In Unesco's publications, lifelong education is usually presented as a 'prospect in education' ; certain theoreticians see in it

a 'state of mind' [1] ; the International Commission on the Development of Education regards it as a principle. It is this last-mentioned definition that we shall use [9, p. 181-182], for of all those proposed it is both the broadest and most specific :

> 'The lifelong concept covers all aspects of education, embracing everything in it, with the whole being more than the sum of its parts. There is no such thing as a separate "permanent" part of education which is not lifelong. In other words, lifelong education is not an educational system but the principle on which the over-all organization of a system is founded, and which should accordingly underlie the development of each of its component parts.'

The conclusions of the Tokyo Conference on adult education, like those of the Grenoble Symposium on short-cycle higher education, and like those of the International Conference on Education, contained an appeal for lifelong education. But they failed to provide a clearer definition of what this meant, and it is precisely this definition that the report of the International Commission offers us. The integration that is desired by all obviously cannot be achieved within the education system whose weaknesses everyone recognizes and which, in any case, was never devised for adults. Neither would it be achieved through the improper extension of the principles of adult education to children of school age. We have, then, to fall back on an over-all education project that will at once cover all ages and meet the needs of adults just as much as those of children or adolescents. Yet recognition of the need for an over-all education project covering the entire span of human life immediately calls for reconsideration of the school's function. How could we impose upon the school, initially established to provide young people with the knowledge, skills and training regarded as sufficient for the whole of their lives, the same obligations when it would be no more than the first stage in an educational process that ends only with life ? Neither its aims nor

1. See, for example : Tardy, M. Reflexions on lifelong integrated education, *Education and culture* (Council of Europe, Strasbourg), No. 3, 1966. See also on this subject, *An introduction to lifelong education,* by Paul Lengrand [13], and the document 'Educational systems and the new demands' prepared by Henri Janne for the International Commission.

its programmes can be the same.[1] But we must also stop confusing lifelong education with adult education. The latter has
certainly introduced the new and imaginative idea of continuity
in education ; however this continuity is not a feature exclusive
to it but common to education as a whole. The education system
of tomorrow, as the International Commission rightly reminds us,
will be something more than the juxtaposition of these two sectors
which are now separate—the school institution on the one hand
and adult education on the other. It will form a single continuous
process, based on the principle of lifelong education.

This principle will therefore never, and by its very nature,
cannot ever be realized in practice, although it will provide the
basis for educational policies, forms of organization and systems.
It is through it and in relation to it that the dialectical tensions
and contradictions experienced at the Tokyo Conference, as at all
recent international meetings devoted to education, can be resolved
into a synthesis valid for all countries in the world, whatever their
level of development.

METHODS AND TECHNIQUES

Although it devoted much of its time to pedagogical matters, the
Tokyo Conference had to admit that our present knowledge
concerning methods and their applicability was still superficial
and fragmentary. It therefore expressed the hope that research
would be developed in this domain and that more frequent international meetings would facilitate exchanges of information on
experiments and innovations. But it established in principle that,
as far as adults were concerned, 'the conventional teacher-student
relationship should become a partnership based on participation
and mutual learning'. In actual fact neither the term 'teacher' nor
the term 'student' are appropriate here, and we continue to use
them simply out of habit and because no suitable substitutes can
be found. But here and there the final report emphasizes the role

1. The collection of texts and bibliographical data published by the
Unesco Institute for Education, Hamburg, under the title *The school and
continuing education* may be consulted on this subject [8].

of organizers, 'animateurs' or intermediaries ('intercessors' is also used sometimes) who help adults to identify their problems, to 'view or listen critically to broadcast programmes' and to determine their reactions. The Conference was very careful to point out the value of self-directed learning for those who prefer to work alone but feel the need for assistance ; it advocated the creation of centres with a friendly atmosphere which they could attend as and when they wished. Here again, research into the specific problems and needs of this kind of education would be desirable. Similarly, due recognition was given to study circles, discussion groups, and organized groups of radio and television programme listeners or viewers, and to the unquestionable effectiveness of instruction by correspondence, particularly at an already advanced level of education.

The question of modern mass communication media provoked the most animated discussion. Had the debate taken place between representatives of the highly industrialized countries there would certainly have been much talk of advanced techniques such as video-cassettes, visio-phones, videodiscs and specially cable television, which has already been piped into millions of homes in the United States and Canada and made its appearance in Europe. But in Tokyo the presence of and the weight carried by the Third World countries inclined to more modesty. Television itself was the subject of fairly sharp criticism. 'Several delegates', we read in the final report, 'voiced concern about the present use of the mass media, especially television. There was a mystique in certain countries about television, that had to be resisted.' As adult education is supposed to welcome innovation, how can this hesitation be explained ? Several Third World countries have, nevertheless, demonstrated considerable boldness in the use of television for educational purposes ; in the Ivory Coast is not the greater part of primary education televised ? Is India not becoming the first country in the world to use a satellite for relaying rural education programmes ?

Criticism was, in fact, levelled mainly at the misuse of television which has been the unfortunate experience of certain countries, particularly in Latin America, due to excessive investments, the unsuitability of imported programmes, high-pressure commercial or publicity methods and intolerable economic constraints.

Whence the praise heaped upon radio broadcasting as being less costly and better designed to reach scattered populations and whence, more especially, the recommendation addressed to the poorest countries to devise 'aids of their own by tapping the rich resources of the community'. This is, in fact, the vast domain—still incompletely explored—of what has come to be called the intermediate technologies, a worthwhile subject for research and, after it has been examined more closely, a useful area for international co-operation.

In the final analysis the Tokyo Conference gave preference to the multi-media approach. Used alone, television and even radio are too 'authoritarian' since they do not allow for feedback ; the passivity of the listener or viewer has the end effect of sapping their enthusiasm. Thus, in order to keep motivation alive and stimulate active participation centred around the reception of messages, those responsible for the organization of the so-called TEVEC experiments in Quebec [12] and, more generally, the advocates of the Open University, have combined radio and television broadcasts with correspondence courses, without neglecting the role of the advisers responsible for maintaining personal contact with each of the adults involved. In stressing the merits of this method which is suitable only at a certain level of initial education, the Tokyo Conference dwelt particularly on the need for the participation of 'animateurs' and on their irreplaceable function and concluded with this particularly important observation : 'Adult educators should therefore reach people in their own natural environment, so that these adults may feel secure and be genuinely motivated.'

ADULT EDUCATION PERSONNEL

This brings us to a consideration of the recruitment, training and status of personnel. The Tokyo Conference was careful to list all the professional categories involved in adult education : 'teachers and instructors, administrators, specialists who prepared education materials such as programmes, films, broadcasts, persons in economic enterprises, extension services in trade unions and co-operative societies . . . . Such a list would also include other professionals who played a significant education role, such as social workers, doctors, religious advisers and persons working in such institutions as libraries, museums and cultural centres.' Although already long, this list is certainly not exhaustive. Why omit artists, writers and performers ? But by trying to be too comprehensive we end up by confusing real adult educators, whose main occupation is education, with occasional collaborators such as doctors, librarians or musicians.

It was these educators proper whom the Conference had in mind when it expressed the hope that a new profession would be established with a status, career prospects, salaries and service conditions 'comparable to those of teachers and administrators in the formal school system'. The Conference rightly made provision for recruitment and training methods for this new profession [3c, p. 34-36]. The idea is most commendable but raises a problem.

It is, of course, perfectly justifiable to attract young, competent, idealistic and devoted people to adult education, to ensure that they enjoy working conditions and salaries commensurate with their functions, and to protect them against insecurity of employment, although it is difficult to go along with the final conclusions of the Tokyo Conference on the subject. Is it really necessary, or even desirable to set up a profession and a body of adult educators ? And is there any point in establishing its status in advance, by situating it at one of the levels of education ? There is considerable danger of creating an additional professional category and of arousing competition, rivalry and possible jealousy ; moreover, an official body, no matter what it is, is always in danger of becoming hidebound. And the teaching profession has so often been reproached with sagging under its own weight ! How would it be possible, once this new profession is organized, to keep adult educators in the same social and cultural environment as their students ? And can we be sure that all the splendid qualities of which adult education advocates are justly proud—such as flexibility, the ability to adjust, a wealth of imagination and a thirst for innovation—would be able to hold their own against the traditions of an established profession ? Admittedly the Conference provided for the maintenance of part-time educators, but are we to understand from this that the Conference was relying on them to keep the torch burning ?

If we look more closely into the question, we are tempted to differentiate between two categories or two functions among adult educators. The first corresponds above all to the need for professional advancement, under clearly defined conditions and in accordance with programmes similar to those of the education system. Although this first function calls for specific skills and methods, which can in any event be acquired through training courses, it does not differ very much from that of teachers, so it is natural that adult educators should be assigned a professional category comparable to that of teachers. On the other hand, when the task is one of providing guidance to a group, under constantly changing conditions and using methods that have to be thought up afresh for each occasion, this function has nothing in common with formal teaching. There are no teachers or students, only equal partners in a jointly prepared project. Would the ideal not be for the organizer himself to be drawn from the group, chosen by unanimous consent for his character and skill in establishing communication ? Such organizers would of course have to be assured of suitable salaries and working conditions, but the choice between that and making them permanently established officials calls for reflexion, and one is inclined to think that the Tokyo Conference has taken the plunge a little too hastily.

But even if we cannot subscribe fully to each of its conclusions, this important gathering in Tokyo was extremely instructive. The volume of information it collected, the sometimes sharp exchanges it produced and the points of agreement that it eventually identified are all to its credit and provide a reassuring picture of the progress achieved by adult education throughout the world.

Chapter five

The Report of the International Commission on the Development of Education

The appearance in the bookshops, in the autumn of 1972, of the report submitted to Unesco by the International Commission on the Development of Education under the promising title *Learning to be* [9] was perhaps not, on the face of it, a memorable event. Yet another volume had been added to the vast literature from all regions of the world on the problems of education today. However, one could not fail to be struck by the names of the authors,[1] all well known in their respective spheres. The forcefulness and boldness of the thought and the cogency of the suggestions addressed to governments and international organizations in this attractive volume were quickly noted. While the book is likely to be of interest to all who give thought to the education of children or adults, it must be borne in mind that it was prepared chiefly in response to a request from the governments of the 130 Member States of Unesco. The result of collective research, it was in addition intended to inspire political decisions and practical measures. Judging from the impact it has made on intergovernmental gatherings, the reactions it has aroused in different countries, one can readily believe that this purpose was largely achieved. The report of the International Commission is now a milestone in the annals of international co-operation.

---

1. Edgar Faure (France), Felipe Herrera (Chile), Abdul-Razzak Kaddoura (Syrian Arab Republic), Henri Lopes (People's Republic of the Congo), Arthur V. Petrovsky (USSR), Majid Rahnema (Iran), Frederick Champion Ward (United States of America).

TERMS OF REFERENCE
AND WORKING METHODS OF THE COMMISSION

In December 1970, the General Conference of Unesco, at its six-teenth session, adopted a resolution whose main operative part reads as follows :

'The Director-General is authorized to prepare and present to Member States the necessary elements for reflection on edu-cational strategies at the international level: ... by establishing an International Commission on the Development of Educa-tion, publishing its report, presenting it with his comments to Member States, the Executive Board, the International Confer-ence on Education and the General Conference, and taking it into consideration in formulating Unesco's future programmes in the field of education.'

Accordingly, at the beginning of 1971 the Director-General set up a commission of seven with Mr. Edgar Faure as its chairman. Three of the seven members had been ministers of education, two occupied prominent positions in institutions devoted to the develop-ment of education, one was a scientist attached to the International Atomic Energy Agency, and one had directed the International Monetary Fund, which finances so many technical assistance pro-jects in education. This team, by reason of the range of professions and the diversity of countries of origin of its members, offered every guarantee that Unesco could hope for. It was assisted by a secretariat of seven. The Commission stated publicly that it had been allowed complete independence in carrying out its terms of reference and complete freedom as regards both the content of its report and the organization of its work.

At its first meeting the Commission had decided to have recourse to various methods. It agreed to : '(a) fact-finding mis-sions to all regions of the world for exchange of views with political leaders and round-table discussions with education author-ities; (b) visits to organizations within the United Nations System, regional institutions and foundations particularly concerned with education problems ; (c) attendance at international and regional meetings ; (d) analysis of documents prepared especially for the Commission by specialists on various aspects of education ; and (e) consultations in executive session with specialists concerning particular educational problems' [9, p. 268].

This promise was kept : twenty-three countries in various regions of the world were visited by Commission members ; meetings with persons in charge of agencies in the United Nations system made it possible to get the major international or regional institutions co-operating in economic and social development to take an interest in the work of the Commission ; but it was chiefly in regard to documentation that the most noteworthy results were achieved. More than eighty studies on the most varied subjects were prepared by well-known experts at the Commission's request. Although these documents are certainly available at Unesco Headquarters or in centres in different parts of the world, it is nevertheless regrettable that the Organization was not in a position to have them more widely circulated, for in many cases they serve to supplement or illustrate the ideas presented in the Commission's report.

On 18 May 1972 the Chairman was able to inform the Director-General of Unesco that the task entrusted to the Commission had been completed and to submit its report to him. This was not to imply, as he was careful to stress, 'that the content of the subject has been exhausted or that its scope would not have justified our spending many more months on further studies or longer reflection'. However, what Unesco wanted was 'not so much an exhaustively erudite study as a critical reflection by men of different origins and background, seeking, in complete independence and objectivity, for over-all solutions to the major problems involved in the development of education in a changing universe' [9, p. *v*].

In view of the tremendous range of the subject, it is amazing that such a short time elapsed between the establishment of the Commission and the submission of the report. Barely seventeen months ! Another remarkable fact is that seven people of such diverse origins and professions were able to reach agreement on complex findings and proposals. It is true that, here and there, footnotes express the reservations of certain members, but these divergencies of opinion are too rare to detract from this striking coincidence of ideas. The unity of tone and style is also admirable, for this collective work flows as smoothly as if it had been written by one and the same author. Concision, coherence and unity are the three characteristics which, from the very outset, impart to this study a persuasive power which is rarely a feature of an international effort.

A CRITICAL REFLECTION

Those who seek in this report objective information on the present
situation of education in the various regions of the world or an
analysis of existing systems and contemplated changes will be
quickly disappointed. The report of the International Commission
is in no way an informative document ; as the Chairman said
so aptly in his Presentation of the report, it is 'a critical reflection'.
This reflection began, of course, with an assessment of the results
obtained by education as it has developed in the world today, an
assessment which leads to a severe verdict, or finding. That is why
Part I of the report bears the thought-provoking title 'Findings'.
Direct references to certain countries or certain facts, and even
statistical data, are of course to be found as we proceed, but these
details are given only by way of example or argument in support
of some theory. In the part entitled 'Innovations and search for
alternatives', which is undoubtedly the most constructive of all,
each of the twenty-one sections opens with the statement of some
'principle', followed by 'Considerata' then a 'Comment', and con-
cludes with an 'Illustration'. Facts are brought in only in order
to give added weight to the demonstration.

A PHILOSOPHY OF EDUCATION

There is no question that this critical reflection was exercised 'in
complete independence', but it is much more difficult to believe it
was exercised 'in complete objectivity'. The tone of the report,
moreover, is not that of an objective research work. If on every
page we detect a note of sincerity, an obvious desire to cast light
on a generally confused subject, it is because we are witnessing
the elaboration of a coherent and logical approach or, as the
Chairman puts it, of 'a dialectical approach comprising, on the one
hand, improvements to be made to existing systems and, on the
other, alternatives to these' [9, p. *xxxiii*].

This feature, depending on the position of the person to whom
the report is directed, is at once its strength and its weakness. In
the eyes of the general public, it is a welcome exception to the
tedious and cautious works usually produced by international

organizations. It continually calls on the reader to join in this critical reflection, in some cases to allow himself to be convinced, in others to raise objections. Few texts are as challenging as this one.

But Unesco was expecting a report which could both serve as a guide for its future action in regard to education and enlighten the governments of Member States seeking solutions to their problems. Is this what is received from the International Commission ? Yes, no doubt, since the report contains recommendations to States and suggestions for the revitalization of international co-operation. However, recommendations and suggestions are all based on the same dialectical approach, which assumes the proportions of an all-embracing philosophy of education. It is all there, from the enunciation of a number of principles to an interpretation of history. It is therefore difficult for governments or Unesco to adopt constructive solutions without at the same time subscribing to the philosophy underlying them.

Most of the principles stated in the report have admittedly long been accepted by intergovernmental bodies concerned with education, such as the Unesco General Conference, the International Conference on Education or the Regional Conferences of Ministers. Such generally-recognized goals as democratization, equality of rights and opportunity, preparation for working life, adult literacy or lifelong education are no longer questioned. The fact that education is ill-suited to the needs of present-day society has become a commonplace. These fundamental principles doubtless received valuable endorsement from the Commission in the form of unusually forceful and convincing illustrations, but governments had already turned them to their advantage and Unesco had already established them as priority goals of its activities.

On the other hand, it is difficult to expect the governments of countries that differ so widely as regards political régime, ideological tendencies and economic development all to adhere to one and the same philosophy of education proposed to them by a group of experts—even if the most eminent and competent in the world ! The philosophy of education and interpretation of history affect the individual cultures and political choices of States too closely. One is reminded of the wise words of warning addressed by Jacques Maritain to Unesco at the very beginning of its existence.

What he said in substance was that no agreement between nations could be based on any ideology or theoretical argument which was likely to divide opinions and, above all, governments. Agreement was possible, however, with a view to practical action.[1] This lesson in pragmatism seems to apply to the Commission's work. Its report would have been more readily acceptable to Member States as a whole and governments would have found it less difficult to adopt its practical recommendations had it not been presented as the outcome of a dialectical approach. True, the report would thereby have lost some of its force. Is it to be regretted that the Commission chose the more difficult path ? However, as international co-operation is essentially pragmatic in character, even when it claims to be based on certain generally-accepted principles, there is hope that once the initial obstacles have been overcome, Unesco and its Member States will be able to distinguish between what is mainly speculation and what leads to constructive action.

FROM THE SCHOOL TO THE LEARNING SOCIETY

The Commission's finding just before it embarks upon its critical reflection is in many respects one of bankruptcy. Despite the tremendous efforts and sacrifices being made, the extension of education and the reforms under way, existing systems meet neither the requirements of democracy nor the basic needs of society. Our education systems are ageing and seizing up. Harsh as this verdict is, it adds nothing to the customary protest against formal education. The question is whether the renovation of the structures of education is enough. In this connexion the Commission reviews the answers put forward by various contemporary schools of thought—from those which credit school with the ability to effect the appropriate changes, to those which vehemently denounce schooling and claim that society must be deschooled. On the face of it, the Commission only advocates a change. However, in an eight-page survey of the universal history of education in primitive societies, as understood by African, Asian, Christian or Islamic tradition and finally in modern times, the Commission

---

1. See the paper by Jacques Maritain in the collection entitled *Human rights : comments and interpretations*. Paris, 1949 [page 10 in particular].

reminds us that education has a far richer past than the relative uniformity of its present structures would lead us to believe. Priceless heritages have been lost or perverted as a result of external forces, especially colonial conquests. Going on to consider present relations between school and society, the shortcomings of programmes, and the inequalities perpetuated by our systems between the children in one and the same country and those of other countries, the report questions the 'fundamental dogma of modern educational systems' according to which schools are the sole fountainhead of education, whereas in fact there are actually more and more centres and sources of education in addition to schools which are more flexible and better suited to our needs. With absolute logic this extensive analysis leads on to the prospect of lifelong education, the main thing being to learn to re-invent and constantly renew, as teaching becomes education and, more and more, learning.

The following passage of paramount importance appears in the Preamble to the report [9, p. *xxxiii*] : 'If learning involves all of one's life, in the sense of both time-span and diversity, and all of society, including its social and economic as well as its educational resources, then we must go even further than the necessary overhaul of "educational systems" until we reach the stage of a learning society. For these are the true proportions of the challenge education will be facing in the future.'

This is the reassuring aspect of the report. For seen in this way, the 'learning society' is the natural setting for lifelong education with all the opportunities it affords of learning, of furthering and supplementing the individual's education and of developing his personality to the full. Other parts of the report, however, contain more provocative statements, which inevitably bring to mind Ivan Illich's famous theories on the learning society—a society in which, apparently, schools have been abolished. [1] For it is a fact that the historical survey which is the point of departure of the critical reflection leads to an implicit condemnation of education as an institution—a condemnation for misappropriation

1. The reference here is to Ivan Illich's book *Deschooling society* [39], and also to the document he prepared for the Commission, 'On the necessity to de-school society'.

of power. Whereas in earlier civilizations it was society as a whole which saw to the education of the young, in Europe, especially since the Renaissance, schools and universities have arrogated to themselves the monopoly of education, raising an artificial barrier between education and society, between educational institutions and life. As Illich repeats over and over again, is not the abolition of schools the surest way of removing this barrier, of opening education to life ?—if that is really what is expected of the learning society.

One must, however, confess to some doubt as to the Commission's real intention. Its Chairman foresaw this danger so clearly that he deemed it necessary to reassure the reader in another passage in the Preamble [9, p. *xxxiii*] :

> 'Admittedly, certain kinds of school and certain forms of teaching must be strongly criticized, if on different grounds for different countries, and many aspects of school education call for thorough-going reappraisal and reformation. Nonetheless, abandoning the idea of school as an essential, if not exclusive, element in education would be tantamount to surrender in the struggle to introduce hundreds of millions of human beings to the kind of education which involves systematic assimilation of knowledge.   And while human culture may not be limited to knowlegde, knowledge remains today an integral and indispensable part of it.'

Will these subtle distinctions suffice to dissipate all fears ? It would be a pity if a few too strongly worded phrases and a somewhat insistent reference to a doctrine that is only too well known were to blind the responsible authorities to the useful advice the Commission has to offer them. The principle of lifelong education has probably never been so forcibly and clearly defended and illustrated as in that part of the report devoted to the learning society ; nor has the indispensable integration of schooling and adult education in one and the same education project.

THE EDUCATION OF THE NEW MAN

In its 'Discoveries' section, and under such evocative headings as 'New findings from research' or 'New developments from science and technology', the report draws attention to the advent of a 'new man' engendered by the scientific and technological revolution. Unlike the industrial revolution of the eighteenth century and the beginnings of mechanization, the scientific and technological revolution, both by virtue of the instantaneous transmission of news over any distance and the invention of computers, has gained supremacy over the minds of mankind as a whole. The new man, the man of the technological era, mass media and cybernetics, needs a new education [9, p. *xxvi*] :

> 'For these reasons the Commission considered that it was essential for science and technology to become fundamental, ever-present elements in any educational enterprise; for them to become part of all educational activities designed for children, young people and adults, so as to help the individual to control not only natural and productive forces, but social forces too, and in so doing to acquire mastery over himself, his choices and actions ; and, finally for them to help man to develop a scientific frame of mind in order to promote the sciences without becoming enslaved by them.'

Here we arrive at one of the climaxes in the Commission's critical reflection and one of the most hotly debated theories. As some delegates had observed at the last session of the International Conference on Education, it is an open question whether people will, in the long run, be content with a culture which is scientific in spirit and technological in substance. These doubts which we so often hear expressed by young people regarding our mechanical civilization, this nostalgia for an existence closer to nature, this anxious quest for the quality of life, along with many other signs, would suggest that the humanism of the future will have to make more room for affective and moral values. Even many scientists confess anxiety at the increasingly dangerous disproportion between the power that scientific progress has given man and his lack of wisdom to master that power and make it serve his happiness. Some even speak of a crisis in science, as if the real crisis were not in man's conscience and in the civilization which he has built up for his own use—a moral and political crisis at the same time. To deal with this crisis, to fulfil the expectations of young people, will it be enough to add still more science and technology to the education or culture of the future ? Are there not other sources that can be drawn on, such as ethical values, creative art or the common store of wisdom and philosophy ? As for the peoples who are as eager to preserve, or even restore, their cultural identity, they can expect no help from science or from the uniformity of technological civilization. This new humanism, which the Commission was so bent upon, will have to accord an important place to the scientific spirit, but we cannot resign ourselves to the idea that it will merely constitute the consecration of the omnipotence of technology. [1]

Since all countries in the world are living in the technological age, the Commission decided not to deal separately with the educational problems of the developing countries. It certainly did not overlook the fact that these countries 'are facing special difficulties and have more stringent obligations than others', for a great many of its recommendations are addressed chiefly to the Third World. However, it had the impression that the broad distinctions drawn as a result of disparities in development 'derived mainly from quantitative evaluations or from practical application'. It then concluded that all countries, developed and underdeveloped alike, would have to 'devise closely comparable strategies, while making use of different means'. Another important question that is discussed time and time again at international gatherings is whether or not the problems posed by education are of the same nature in the Third World as in the industrialized countries. On the highest level, the philosophical level, the similarities predominate, but as one comes nearer to realities, the differences—not only quantitative but also qualitative—become more apparent. As the report says, there is probably not a single human being who is unable to listen in to a transistor radio, but it would be better if all human beings possessed a radio and there was a message to receive. Where there is nothing, or practically nothing, of what avail is the most sophisticated technology in the world ? This important point will remain at issue until all peoples, in all countries, have reached a comparable educational level.

EDUCATION STRATEGIES

It is on this point that the Commission's conclusions were so eagerly awaited. According to the terms of reference it received

1. See the autumn 1973 and summer 1974 issues of the review *Prospects* [17].

from Unesco, the intention was that its report would assist governments to formulate national strategies for the development of education ; it would propose criteria and would outline 'a methodology which governments could use to evolve national strategies suited to the different situations and to the different development objectives'. The Commission was also expected to produce 'a typology based on certain major regional or national features'.

Were these terms of reference too ambitious ? Was it too much to ask of a group of eminent experts, but individuals whose time was strictly limited ? We can tell that certain governments have been somewhat disappointed. They would be wrong to complain, however, for despite the absence of a typology which would have been extremely useful and which still remains to be drawn up, Part III of the report offers them, spread over some sixty pages, 'elements for contemporary strategies' which are sufficiently clear and detailed for useful lessons to be drawn from them.

To begin with, the Commission clarifies the meaning to be attributed to the somewhat muddled term of 'strategy', as applied to education, by distinguishing three stages in the decision-making process : the initial stage, which is the adoption of an education *policy*, or in other words, the basic choices, followed by the *strategic* stage whose object is to 'transcribe policy into a body of conditional decisions, determining action to be taken in relation to different situations which may arise in the future'. The last stage is one of *planning*, the purpose of which is to 'make decisions easier at the various levels where strategical directives must be applied. It does this by making the calculations required to quantify the terms of technical choices and by taking care that all necessary factors brought together when the time comes to take action'.

The Commission had foreseen that these definitions might be 'somewhat forbidding'. It is rather their lack of clarity that we reproach, and a few specific examples would not have been amiss. It is quite clear what education policy is, and for a long time now most States have applied themselves to planning. It is the intermediate stage—the 'central link in the chain', that of strategy—which is most difficult to make out clearly. The Commission lays emphasis, however, on the logical process which, moving from policy to strategy and from strategy to planning, ensures the

continuity and relevance of decisions made from one level to the
next ; it is even, in its view, the failure to adhere to this logical
process that 'is responsible for education having been too often
oriented by chance, guided blindly and developed in anarchic
fashion' [9, p. 169-172].

FROM LINEAR EXPANSION
TO ALTERNATIVE EDUCATIONAL STRATEGIES

Everything becomes clear when, moving from definitions to their
applications, the Commission undertakes a convincingly damning
analysis of the strategies adopted during the past fifteen years
in a large number of countries in the Third World. These strategies
were, in fact, based on a 'linear expansion' of systems and the
numbers of people involved. By this we understand the quantitative development of a system according to the lines of its earlier
evolution, each level of schooling continuing along its course by
simple extrapolation of its past trends. This system programmes
educational needs as a direct function of forecasts of student flows,
and of the potential for expansion of the different elements of
the school system : buildings, equipment, teaching staff. These
purely quantitative programming methods can be applied to relatively stable systems in the course of steady expansion, as in the
most developed countries.

Yet in the case of countries that are confronted by tremendous
needs and rapidly changing situations, 'no mechanical extrapolation can now yield valid forecasts of developments in such a
dynamic and living enterprise as education'. We see that quantitative expansion of education systems does not go hand in hand
with efficient education ; 'enormous financial and human
resources were laid out to develop costly school models, the results
of which often fell far short of expectations'. Linear expansion
is thus responsible for the poor efficiency of education and for
most of the disappointments suffered by many of the developing
countries.

This verdict is far-reaching : it condemns both the ill-advised
importation of foreign models and the strategies so far adopted
on the basis of these models. But the Commission does not confine

itself to negative criticism. It proposes at the same time that 'strategies must be modified, must move from the quantitative to the qualitative, from imitation and reproduction to a search for innovations, from a uniform procedure to diverse alternatives'. And we should emphasize the two key words, *alternatives* and *innovations,* which designate the two concepts on which the Commission bases the dynamics of the new education.

AN APPROACH TO THE PROBLEM OF CHANGE

The aim of educational reform may be to change or improve what already exists ; this is most frequently the case. But in present circumstances, taking possibilities and experience already gained into account, the Commission considers that reforms of this kind will not in general be adequate, even if they are major ones. Alternatives must be sought to what exists, as regards both the very concepts and structures of education. There is no longer any question of improving, but of innovating, for alternative strategy demands constant recourse to innovation.

It is at this point that we may regret the absence, in this report, of a real methodology on which governments could have based their policies and more especially their strategies. It would seem that the Commission has shown preference not for a systematic approach but a problem-based one which, while laying down clearly defined principles, leaves it to the authorities to consider the most appropriate solution for each situation. For obviously there is no universal strategy that can be applied in all countries and all circumstances ; there are only national strategies.

The Commission draws attention to two diametrically opposed pitfalls, both of which must be avoided. First it is no longer desirable to embark on changes in piecemeal fashion, without a concept of the totality of the goals and modes of the educational process, and envisaging their consequences—which excludes both improvisation and pragmatism. Real change is that which affects the system as a whole, both now and in the future. But, from another aspect, neither must we 'dare nothing, fail to grasp new possibilities or commit ourselves to tomorrow ... we must think clearly in exploring new paths for the future'.

The twenty-one principles that the Commission presents in the subsequent part of its report, and supports with numerous comments and illustrations, constitute the framework of an approach to the problem, from the general principle of lifelong education with, as corollary, the diversification of means, in time as in space, and the 'deformalization' of institutions, to the ultimate principle of the learner's responsibilities, and covering all levels of education and all forms of education for young people and adults. We see then that the approach conceived by the Commission is heavily weighted by fundamental policy choices : democratic education, both in and out of school, making wide use of modern technologies and all social forces, substituting the idea of learning for that of education at every stage in life. To put this in a nutshell, education must be 'conceived of as a process in the human being, who thereby learns to express himself, to communicate and to question the world, through his various experiences, and increasingly—all the time—to fulfil himself'. Hence the title of the report : *Learning to be.*

To round off its discussion of the issue of change, the Commission has outlined the 'ways and means' for the execution of educational strategies : identifying, stimulating and experimenting with innovations; highly decentralized administration and management, implying learner participation, the joint management of institutions and even their autonomous management ; the search for new and more varied means of financing education. However imaginative this part of the report may be, it is unfortunately confined to suggesting broad trends. We would like to have heard more about the 'networks for change', capable of multiplying their effects or producing them through a kind of echo effect ; more especially, we would like to have been better informed about methods calculated to reduce costs without affecting the quality of education. In this instance, as in many others, the Commission no doubt was pressed for time but it has to be admitted that its suggestions would have been more telling and convincing had they been more explicit. The Commission is to be supported wholeheartedly when it denounces the waste of financial and human resources due to traditional linear expansion strategies, although it is difficult not to ask whether alternative educational strategies would not impose on States, particularly those of the Third World, admittedly with more constructive results, sacrifices out of proportion to their resources ? Once again the crucial question of the financing of education is left without any conclusive reply.

NATIONAL STRATEGIES
AND INTERNATIONAL CO-OPERATION

Since education is, by its nature, a national matter, closely linked with the culture, society and level of development peculiar to each country, and since imitation of foreign models has always proved disappointing and often disastrous, what is the role of international co-operation to be ? It is to the great credit of the Commission that it raises this question without beating about the bush. The oldest form of co-operation that takes the form of exchanges, between countries, of information, teachers and students, is available to all States, whatever their level of development. It is more necessary than ever at a time when there is a need 'to rethink educational systems, to study the manifold aspects of educational theory and practice, to compare problems and their solutions'.

More recently another form of co-operation has emerged, namely, international aid to education, which has two major justifications. The first is that 'since the expanding need for education is out of all proportion to the resources available for meeting it, many developing countries lack even the means to continue the already intense effort they are making in this direction, without running the risk of entirely exhausting their budgets'. Secondly, 'international aid may greatly facilitate innovation. Most countries hesitate to venture into new areas for fear of gambling away their already inadequate resources. Others who make up their minds to do it can frequently go no further without outside financial help'. In support of this argument the Commission cites the precedent of the Green Revolution, which owed its success to continuing assistance from foreign sources. Unlike the first type of co-operation, which relies mainly on human resources, the second demands financial investments over a fairly long period.

Having stated these premises, the Commission goes on to assess the results achieved by international co-operation on a bilateral basis, through country-to-country agreements, and on a multilateral basis, through the activities of the United Nations and its specialized agencies, Unesco in particular. The verdict is harsh :

'Co-operation in education is currently in the throes of a crisis similar to that running through all international aid. This may be seen from the obstacles aid is facing all over the world : the diminution in the percentage of GNP which some of the world's most developed countries are devoting to it, the dead ends in which many developing countries now find themselves and the broadsides of criticism currently being fired by both giving and receiving nations. The first group attacks wastage and inefficiency, the second complains of attempts to gain political, strategic or commercial advantage, and to impose foreign cultural models, under the cover of external assistance' [9, p. 236].

Although sombre, the picture is nonetheless accurate. In matters of co-operation, the reproach concerning waste and inefficiency is heard only too often at major international gatherings, where speakers have no hesitation in accusing the countries that participate most actively in international aid of 'neocolonialism'. As to the causes of the crisis, the Commission points mainly to the inadequacy of aid, the economic counterparts required by the donors in the form of 'tied aid', the proliferation of experts, often badly trained for their task and the dispersion of projects which are too piecemeal to bring about the transformation of obsolete systems.

This gloomy analysis is not intended to challenge the need for co-operation which, fortunately, is developing and must be developed further. The Commission emphasizes that 'an essential fact in the contemporary world is the feeling of solidarity' ; but something must be done to trace out the paths leading to this solidarity. All members of the Commission agree on the negative side of the diagnosis : 'neither the forms of present bilateral and multilateral aid nor the resources available to it—and even the concepts which inspire it—are equal to the educational needs confronting the international community.' The courage must be found to rethink, from top to bottom, the whole system of international co-operation. On the other hand, when the members of the Commission came to examine possible remedies for this state of affairs, we learn from the report that they were divided into two different schools of thought : (a) according to some, it is not necessary to create new programmes, centres or funds, but to re-organize and re-distribute programmes, centres and existing means in a new way, so that they correspond more closely to educational needs in the years to come ; (b) others conceived a solution which would appear to deserve attention, i.e. to launch an international programme aimed solely at providing scientific, technical and financial aid for States wishing to embark upon new educational strategies.

As the first of these two remedies is confined to an expression of pious hopes, too vague to generate any action, there is no other way forward for those who put their faith in the Commission, than the international programme for educational innovation.

THE REACTIONS OF STATES TO THE COMMISSION'S REPORT

During 1972 and 1973, Unesco's Member States had three separate opportunities to express their views on the Commission's report. The General Conference, at its seventeenth session in Paris in October and November 1972, had before it the report, which was introduced by the Chairman of the Commission, and embarked upon a full discussion of the subject. Generally speaking, the report was warmly received. Most delegations paid tribute to the study carried out and expressed their conviction that the Commission's work would make a valuable contribution both to the future action of governments and to international co-operation. As was to be expected, rather serious reservations were also expressed. At the conclusion of the debate, the Conference invited Member States :

'(a) to examine the guidelines and recommendations of the Commission and to communicate their conclusions to the Director-General for submission to the International Conference on Education at its XXXIVth session ;

(b) to undertake experiments or to proceed with activities under way with the aim of studying certain basic issues which could make a contribution to educational reform and to the development of educational strategies ; and to make available to the Director-General the evaluation of results achieved ;

(c) to organize, with assistance from Unesco and possibly from

other organizations, national, sub-regional and regional meetings and, if need be, meetings of an international character,
to study further the recommendations of the Commission and
to determine ways and means of implementing them at the
national level.' [1]

The appeal by the General Conference seems to have aroused
interest in many countries. *Learning to be* has been translated into
six languages, and contracts were signed in 1973 for its publication
in twelve other languages. At about the same date seminars
devoted specifically to an examination of the report were held in
some ten countries ; others have certainly been organized since.
Records of their proceedings, like those of the discussions of the
International Conference on Education held at Geneva in September 1973, reveal the interest aroused throughout the world by
the Commission's contribution and the importance that many States
attach to it. However, we are still far from general agreement
on all the recommendations in the report, and as dissenting opinions are, in such cases, more thought-provoking than points of
agreement, it is those opinions that should be singled out for
attention.

Although they do not challenge the desirability of a continual
improvement of education, certain countries—always the same
ones—reject the pessimistic verdict of the Commission on the
present state of education, at least as far as they themselves are
concerned. Others, more numerous, stating that they wish to bring
about radical changes in existing systems, are disturbed by the
implicit condemnation of the school as an institution, which they
firmly support. For yet others, the relationship between education
and the social and economic structures appears to have been
studied too superficially. The prospect of a learning society, in the
view of many, seems to be a Utopian idea rather than a realistic
and attainable objective. In general, some of the basic concepts
used by the Commission seem too vague to serve as a guide for
constructive action. Several countries which reproach the report
with being too optimistic about the anticipated benefits of science

---

1. See : Unesco. *Records of the General Conference, seventeenth
session, Paris 1972.* Vol. 1 : *Resolutions, Recommendations.* Paris, 1973.
p. 20.

and technology, would prefer the education of young people to be centred on reasonable attitudes based on respect for human dignity and concern for the preservation of nature. Although agreement on the principle of lifelong education is easy to achieve, doubts are expressed whether the report is likely to make any useful contribution to the practical application of this imaginative idea. Lastly, it is regretted by many that the Commission, in proposing universal principles for the education of tomorrow, gives the impression of confusing the modernization of education systems with recourse to Western technologies.

This brief summary of the main objections expressed so far with regard to the report *Learning to be* confirms certain reservations that we ourselves have made during the course of this study. They prove, more than anything else, the extent to which it is difficult for critical thinking on the problem of education to enlist the general support of widely differing countries when it is based on abstract considerations and concepts which are not readily grasped by all cultures. But did the Commission really set out to convince its readers ? Was it not content to provoke reactions, by inducing the responsible authorities to embark upon some genuine heart searching ?

There remain the two final conclusions of the report. Is recourse to innovations really the supreme remedy advocated by the Commission for the crisis in education ? Does the crisis that the Commission believes it has detected in international co-operation justify implementation of a world programme for innovations ?

Chapter six

Priority to innovation

Like the word 'strategy', the term 'innovation' only recently gained currency in the language of educational theorists, but it has rapidly become extremely popular ; international organizations, such as OECD and Unesco, lost no time in seizing upon it. It is bandied about in the press, and a flourishing literature has grown up around this concept. It is far from true, however, that the ideas suggested by this term have already attained a satisfactory degree of clarity. So, before weighing up the chances for an international programme for educational innovation, such as that which the International Commission on the Development of Education suggested should be launched, it is important to reach agreement on a few basic points, such as what innovation really is and how it comes about, or, indeed, what necessary conditions must be fulfilled before an innovation which has succeeded in one country may be of use to other countries.

THE NATURE OF INNOVATION

The word innovation connotes change, but is not synonymous with it. All changes made in educational structures or practices, or all breaks with custom, do not necessarily constitute innovations as the theorists understand the term. The report of the Edgar Faure Commission constantly warns us against the temptations of improvisation and pragmatism ; a certain innovation implies a considered intention, a clearly-conceived objective, and sufficient firmness of purpose to bring about a profound and lasting improvement.

Choosing from among all the definitions which have been put forward, we shall therefore settle for one to be found in a study carried out under the auspices of OECD, i.e., 'those attempts at change in an educational system which are consciously and purposefully directed with the aim of improving the present system' [23, p. 13].

There is no lack of examples to support this definition. The immediate aim of countries which introduced the new maths into primary and secondary education was to give a fresh slant to curricula in order to make them more readily assimilable ; but it was also their intention to use this as a means of attracting more young people to the science side ; taking an even longer view, they hoped to bring about changes in relationships between teachers and pupils through a more active educational policy. Thus a limited innovation was expected to produce far-reaching changes in the education system as a whole. Conversely, the circumstances in which Freinet had deliberately placed himself did not allow his innovatory methods to influence State schools, from which he held himself aloof, nor even private education, which was unable to follow his lead. But, much later, in the service of research undertaken in the framework of the school establishment, the same methods provided inspiration for a reform which is expected to have very far-reaching effects. This points to the conclusion that a new and well thought-out idea does not always result in a genuine innovation.

PROCESSES OF INNOVATION

From North America, in the nineteen-sixties, came the idea of applying industrial innovation techniques to education. The bustling energy of American life, both in Canada and the United States, the progress of technology and the free enterprise system compelled industry to be constantly on the look-out for new ideas. Meanwhile, some observers, economists and sociologists, grew irritated to see education—which had, after all, become one of the greatest achievements of modern life—settling into entrenched attitudes which they considered antiquated. In order to catch up with and keep abreast of modern developments, educators therefore had no alternative but to start looking for change too, by means of innovation strategies. These ideas, spread about by theorists and taken up by educational specialists, found particularly striking expression in the conclusions of the Conference held in Williams-burg, in 1967, on the World Education Crisis. [1]

In the United States, most of the studies in the process of inno-vation are therefore based on the industrial model : first research, followed by development of its findings, followed by distribution to the public of the new product. The same goes for innovation in education, which must follow the same blueprint, whose pattern has become standard : research and development. [2] Other theorists, aware of the exceptional complexity of the educational process, are introducing a variation, choosing rather to take their models from agriculture, in which changes are less rapid than in industry and more often encounter the resistance of forces of habit ; but, in its essentials, the pattern remains the same.

This manner of treating education as if it were on a par with the products of industry or agriculture is likely to offend many thinkers. When a new industrial model has been perfected, for example, a car, a television set or a washing machine, it can be mass-produced by machinery, and the quality of the individual item maintained ; however, in the same country and even in the same town, the same curricula and the same methods practised by different teachers with different pupils seldom produce identical results.   Teachers and pupils are not machines, but human beings, with all the diversity and uncertainties inherent in human nature. The concept of educational quality, which is funda-mental to the thinking of educators, has always thrown economists off balance. It is encouraging to find some American theorists of innovation issuing a timely warning in this connexion [28]. It is in the world of education itself, then, that models must be sought, not, indeed, in order to cut off the school from its social or

1. See the well-known book by Philip H. Coombs (*The world educa-tional crisis*, New York, N.Y., Oxford University Press, 1968), and the studies by Ladislav Cerych and Alexander King, prepared for the Williams-burg Conference.

2. A perfect illustration of this pattern is to be found in the book by E.M. Rogers and F.F. Shoemaker [44].

economic surroundings, but simply in order to remain attuned to its specific character and its own terms. This method was very successfully adopted by the experts appointed by OECD to examine the process of innovation in education [23].

With this reservation, the 'research and development' pattern is still of value. In the United States, the Federal Government, like the universities and private establishments, is devoting considerable sums of money to research and experiment prior to reform. For example, the new departure in mathematics teaching cost $US5 million in two years, and an equal amount was spent on physics teaching. A similar pattern is also to be observed in the Soviet Union, where the academics of the educational sciences are responsible for conducting research and experiments intended to prepare the way for reforms in each Republic or throughout the Union. Educational research is beginning to flourish on an unprecedented scale throughout the world, as the periodical reports from the various States confirm.

However, one should not attach too much weight to the part played by research in the planning of changes. Examples abound of reforms decreed by legislation without preliminary research, either under the pressures of a sudden crisis, like the one which occurred in France in the spring of 1968, or in the context of a political project of much broader scope, like the Soviet reform of education adopted in 1958. Conversely, it is surprising that the universally known and appreciated work of Jean Piaget on child psychology and the origins of the acquisition of knowledge should have had only a slight influence on the tendencies of reforms decreed by the public authorities. The relationship is still too vague between research and decision-making and between research and school practice. If the research centres were placed in direct contact with the schools, at every level, this would be a great step forward. The moves made in this direction by some countries thus seem all the more admirable, such as the setting up of the Council for Innovation in Education in Norway, that of the National Committee of Education in Sweden, or the Schools Council in the United Kingdom.

Will this new importance attached to research in the innovation process render abortive individual attempts at innovation by teachers or educational establishments ? Many signs indicate that the age of pioneers is over. The days are gone when a Montessori, a Decroly, or a Dewey could, by sheer force of example, set off chain reactions. Even in countries where education is largely decentralized, the State has become so acutely aware of its responsibilities, the problems of education have become so central to political activity and the economy exerts such heavy pressure on the careers of young people, that a reform, even if restricted to a particular aspect of education, is likely to set all the wheels of public authority in motion. However, in the modest performance of his daily task, the personality of the teacher is of more importance nowadays that ever it was, and imagination and the ability to accept new ideas are even more ncessary to him. Even in the smallest schools, minor innovations may be made which remain unpublicized, but which nevertheless contribute to progress in teaching. It is surely possible to think up another process for innovation apart from the kind which passes through the channels of systematically organized research in special establishments, a process which would take place entirely at the school, thanks to the energy of one person—headmaster of teacher—or group of persons who have joined forces in pursuit of a common objective, and thanks to the infectious power of example. Although Freinet did not succeed in his time in making much impression on the education system of his country, he eventually claimed so many disciples by his example that the time has come at last when methods bearing his name have received the official stamp of approval in the form of ministerial directives. One can never predict the future of an innovation that orginated at the grass-roots level.

Moreover, these two patterns are not mutually exclusive : research must feed on teaching experience, just as the creative power of the teacher must look for support in the findings of research. This presupposes a constant flow of information, especially at the experimental stage. A good example of such fruitful co-operation is provided by the method which has been adopted in France, in the past ten years, to reform the teaching of the French language at primary school. On the basis of a working hypothesis, devised by a team of experts after lengthy work on linguistics and contemporary psychology, a major operational research campaign was conducted throughout France, in both urban and rural areas. Teams of volunteers were set up at 90 key points in the country, with the participation of 950 primary school-teachers, heads of schools and teachers of teacher-training colleges, educational advisers and school psychologists, as well as specialists in linguistics. The teams communicated with one another by means of a liaison bulletin ; provisional reports on on-going experiments were published at intervals by the Institut National de Recherche et de Documentation Pédagogiques (INRDP). So, gradually, with research and experiment developing hand in hand, the project finally resulted in a ministerial directive towards the end of 1972—the first step in the implementation of a long-awaited reform.[1] This is a good example—all too rare, alas—of close collaboration among researchers, teachers and decision-making bodies.

RESISTANCE TO INNOVATION

Circumstances are more favourable now than ever before to the spirit of innovation. The speed of progress in science and technology, the mobility of the needs of the economy and the resulting instability in employment, the uncertainty reigning over the future of society and even of our entire civilization, the challenging of values hitherto considered unassailable, and the changes which physiology and psychology are revealing in the development and behaviour of adolescents in a school environment : all these things contribute to our impression that we are being carried along by an irresistible current which is bearing us to an unknown destination. Obviously, education must keep pace with this movement and attempt to give it meaning. But the theorists of innovation are always saying that the education system resists the trend with the dead weight of inertia, and that it is proving to be both incapable of changing itself and even unable to tolerate reforms. In the eyes of public opinion, education is often a scapegoat. It would be as unwise to overlook these rumblings of discontent as it would be to pay too much attention to them. It is certain that a misunderstanding is growing up between the world of education and the rest of society; this is only one of the more obvious symptoms of what has been called the world education crisis.

1. See nos. 38, 44, 47 and 61, published between 1968 and 1973, of the periodical *Recherches pédagogiques,* published in Paris by INRDP.

To the extent that it is an establishment, founded by laws and ruled by custom, education is naturally inclined to stability, in the same way as other establishments such as the legal profession, the army, parliaments or churches. But education is also a great living organism, whose health depends on the harmony achieved among its various members : the civil service, the teaching profession and that vast multitude of young people who are its reason for existing. There are also the families, which surround it and observe it from all angles, and which are nothing less than the nation itself.

In any field, the civil service always tends to take a stranglehold. In highly centralized countries, its weight is to be felt everywhere, and as it is farthest away from down-to-earth everyday reality, its action also becomes slower and more rigid. Many people use this argument to support their claim that innovation stand fewer chances of success under centralized régimes. On the other hand, once a decision for change has been made, it is implemented more rapidly throughout the country. In countries with a broadly decentralized system, the administrative machinery is less ponderous and is in closer contact with reality, so that it can act with greater flexibility and give more scope to the schools and the teachers, but it is also more vulnerable to pressure from powerful individuals in local politics or with private interests. When innovation depends on a host of local bodies, which often cannot see eye to eye, progress is slow and obstacles are plentiful—to such an extent that there seems to be little to choose between the two systems. It is nevertheless true that an ill-formed or unco-operative civil service can oppose stubborn resistance to the planning and implementation of innovations. It is a force to be reckoned with ; the legislator must work to bring it under control.

As for the pupils and students, who form the vast majority of partners in the educational enterprise, they submitted for a long time to the law of the establishment and were unable and unwilling to alter it. But things have changed a good deal. Even under the most authoritarian régimes, young people in universities and schools are succeeding in making their voices heard ; sooner or later, authority has to take them into account. In many countries, as we have seen in this study, students are now expected to take an active part in the management of universities ; in secondary schools, pupils often sit on governing boards, side by side with their teachers and with delegates from their families. We can rely on young people to encourage innovations, even if they do not always recognize which of these are the soundest.

TEACHERS AND INNOVATION

The attitude of the teaching profession is what ultimately determines the success or failure of an innovation. Many people say that teachers are naturally hostile to change. Is this true ? One of the merits of the OECD report, which we have already had occasion to quote, is that it tackles this question quite straightforwardly [23, p. 42]. It recalls that teachers, owing to their high intellectual level, are more inclined than other people to be critical, particularly of new ideas. Their resistance, where it occurs, would appear to be deep-rooted : on a psychological level, they tend to reject innovations which threaten their security ; on a practical level, they demand proof which education theory is unable to provide ; on a professional level, they see changes originating from outside as an encroachment on their field of competence and are irritated to see amateurs taking decisions without consulting them and without foreseeing the difficulties they will raise.

Such a painstaking analysis is very creditable, but those who have spent a long time, in a professional capacity, observing teachers, and who have often been taken into their confidence, will wish to correct it in some respects. First, as regards security. Nowadays, if one feeling predominates among school-teachers, it tends to be insecurity : insecurity towards their pupils, their families, public opinion and, above all, their responsibilities. In the past, a teacher was self-reliant, alone in front of his class and alone with his conscience ; today, he feels the need to be more strongly supported and better equipped to carry out his demanding job. He wants facilities for further training and opportunities for retraining ; this is now one of the constant demands of the teaching profession, especially among its younger members.

It is true that this body of people has a more highly-developed critical faculty than others, and yet nowadays the most trivial educational dispute takes on the proportions and the tone of a holy war. So much strong feeling and taking of sides is involved that the critical spirit is often submerged. It is unfortunate that the most sophisticated educational theory is still not in a position to furnish concrete proof of an innovation's effectiveness. Taking stock of the research done in this field is a dispiriting exercise. Whether in reading, mathematics or foreign languages, little difference is to be found between the results obtained by various methods. Perhaps this failure should be put down to flaws in the yardsticks of assessment, since the tests in use in our education system are all too often based on academic results and do not attach enough importance to the evaluation of attitudes. Perhaps, too, we are in the habit of relying on averages, whereas reactions to change are also influenced by educational standards, family backgrounds and the environment. Whatever the reasons behind this powerlessness, we must join with a writer who in nevertheless staunchly in favour of innovations in acknowledging that 'a comparison between active methods and traditional methods, which is often made in the United States and in Great Britain, does not point to a categorical conclusion in favour of either the former or the latter, if only the traditional academic results are taken into account'. [1]

It is undoubtedly possible to claim, as this writer does, that it is the innovation itself which is important, because of the upsurge of creativity involved and the energy mobilized. It will be readily admitted that, as he says, 'the very process of innovation is a factor of productivity' and that it is for this reason that 'it is important to give it constant encouragement'.

In other words, the value of innovation resides above all in its intrinsic virtues, its power to provoke within the system what the American Rogers calls 'a continuing and constructive turmoil' or, alternatively, to generate a spirit of innovation [32]. One can scarcely fail to acknowledge, however, with Eurich, that it is meaningless to seek change for its own sake, just as it is to reject indiscriminately the tried and tested methods merely for the pleasure of adopting new ones. One would run the risk of banish-

---

1. See the work by Jean Hassenforder, *L'innovation dans l'enseignement* [34, p. 113-115]. The author takes as his principle basis the work of the English sociologist Michael Young and that of J.M. Stephens and R.W. Tyler in the United States.

ing one orthodoxy only to set up another in its place [28, p. 105]. Education cannot tolerate too frequent changes ; introducing a reform without taking the time to observe the results of the previous one, as we so often see happening in countries such as France, is perhaps a way of keeping people's minds alert, but is a surer way of creating chaos. What ultimately matters is not the number or the frequency of the changes, but the order in which they occur and the co-ordination of their effects in the light of the chosen objective. We always come back to the wise counsel of the International Commission : where innovation is concerned, steer clear of both improvisation and pragmatism.

These factors, perhaps, justify the suspicious attitude of the teaching profession. Its resistance can be overcome only by associating it, at every stage, in the planning of changes. It may seem surprising that in Sweden, after a long series of research projects, consultations and public debates, when Parliament had finally adopted a general reform of education, to all appearances a model of its kind, the teachers went on strike to prevent it from being implemented. In this particular instance, the teachers, who had had a chance to express their views like everyone else, were clearly in the wrong and it was quite right to implement the reform in spite of them. But we must join with Torsten Husén in admitting that, nearly always, events unfold as if a decision has been made to act *on* the teachers, for them no doubt, but never with them. This is an attitude of technocratic paternalism, based on mistrust, which in turn causes the teaching profession to reject the reformer in such a case, just as a living organism rejects the transplant imposed on it by the surgeon [32, p. 133]. A constant flow of information between summit and base and, conversely, between base and summit, so as to enable the competent authorities to appreciate the obstacles and difficulties ; close communication between the centres for research and experiment, on the one hand, and schools and teachers on the other ; the active participation of teachers and, wherever possible, of those taught and their families, in consultations prior to decisions—these are the most favourable conditions for an innovation to be widely adopted.

Lastly, whatever the system, whether centralized or not at the decision-making level, it must respect the pedagogical autonomy of the teacher. Once the objectives of a reform have been clearly set out, and once general guidelines have been laid down for achieving those objectives, the teachers must be trusted, each in his class and all together in their school, working under the authority of the head of the establishment, to adapt the change to local conditions and circumstances—to the natural, social and cultural surroundings and to the aptitudes and aspirations of the pupils. Even under a centralized régime, there is nothing to be gained from attempting to bring about a situation in which everywhere, in each establishment, the same timetables and curricula are rigidly adhered to, the same methods used and the same exercises carried out. On the contrary, much will be lost, for this is the way to stifle imagination, repress creative spontaneity and clip the wings of the spirit of innovation. To substitute diversity for uniformity and free initiative for conformism : these should be the guiding principles of vocational training for future teachers.

THE TRANSFER OF INNOVATIONS

With the transition from the national context to that of international co-operation, fresh difficulties come to light. When encouraging States to adopt innovation strategies, how can one avoid offering them models which were never designed for their use ? Many of the innovations generally considered to be the most valuable call for funds which are to be had in only a few countries : the 'Parkway Programme' for example, in Philadelphia, or the one which was recently launched in Chicago. As we know, a common feature of these innovations is that pupils meet only in small groups and for a few hours a week, the rest of their time being spent outside the school, in establishments freely chosen by them which fit the curriculum adopted for them : libraries, museums, newspaper offices, radio or television stations, cinema studios or even, on occasion, the law courts. The Parkway Programme began in 1968 with 140 pupils, and this figure had risen to 700 by the following year. The famous 'university-without-walls', which links 20 or so associated colleges around Antioch College in the State of Ohio, and the one which was established on the same principles in New York, had approximately 2,000 students in 1972, all doing individual work [36]. The initiators of these experiments are certainly to be admired for their ingenuity and audacity, but one should not close one's eyes to the fact that the experiments are expensive, that they are aimed at limited numbers of pupils and that they cannot develop without the vast cultural resources provided by large towns such as Philadelphia, Chicago or New York. All these conditions rule out the possibility of holding them up as examples to less well-equipped countries. Expensive, too, is the lengthy research leading up to the adoption of educational innovations in the United States, in Scandinavia or in the Soviet Union. There is a need for strong financial backing and establishments which are well endowed with highly competent personnel.

Another difficulty is connected with the uncertainty which continues to overshadow the medium- or long-term results to be expected from many innovations. If, in a single country, educational experiments prove incapable of demonstrating the greater efficiency of any one method over others, there seem to be few good arguments for recommending other countries to try it when they cannot afford to embark on risky experiments. International transfer of innovations is not a foolproof undertaking. From country to country, spontaneous phenomena are certainly to be observed, and these may be attributed to the infectiousness of example : for instance, the introduction and widespread adoption of the new maths in primary and secondary schools, or the use of direct methods and audio-visual aids in the teaching of modern languages. It is this power of example which must be set to work systematically to foster an innovatory attitude throughout the world.

By example I do not mean model. Nothing could be more disastrous or counter-productive than to encourage imitations. Repeating the same innovation, on the pretext that it has succeeded in another country, in different circumstances and with resources which bear no comparison, would lead the way to a sort of educational neo-colonialism. On the contrary, a questing and creative frame of mind must be encouraged and sustained, both in national education authorities and among the multitudes of teachers and educators of adults. The road of international co-operation, especially with regard to the developing countries, seems therefore to be both straight and narrow.

AN INTERNATIONAL PROGRAMME
FOR INNOVATION

Concluding its examination of the report submitted by the Edgar
Faure Commission, the International Conference on Education has
already produced some useful statements. Having recalled the
fundamental principle that 'each country would have to ultimately
develop the competence to discover for itself the unique innovations needed for the continual regeneration of its education' and
that this was a national task, the Conference nevertheless took the
view that 'it could, however, be considerably assisted by a clearing-
house service run by Unesco at the international level'. Lastly,
it stated that such a service could 'provide information, documentation, opportunities and assistance for further study in depth,
and technical assistance for the preparation of project design'
[4i, p. 13].
    These brief indications point to three possible types of service :
(a) exchange of information intended to provide examples of innovations ; (b) system of reference designed to facilitate the extensive
studies which every country must carry out in order to invent its
own necessary innovations ; (c) technical assistance to help each
country to plan and implement the innovations.

Exchange of information

Unquestionably, the International Bureau of Education (IBE) is the
best qualified and best equipped to provide, in Unesco's name, a
two-way international clearing-house service, from the centre to
the periphery and from the periphery to the centre. As the
examples most likely to spark off new experiments are those which
originate in nearby, similar countries, exchange should take place
first of all within a single region, operating through national
documentation centres, whose establishment in each of its Member
States Unesco has long been trying to encourage, and the regional
offices which it maintains in each of the regions of the world. In
the second stage of the process, the two-way flow of information
might be extended to all Member States, so that the IBE would thus
become the centre of a network destined eventually to cover the
whole world.

Thought should also be given to the various categories of recipients of such information. Naturally, the supreme education authorities are those which must be won over to the cause of innovations—those which take decisions or prepare the ground for them, either at the national level in countries with a centralized régime or, in the other countries, the provincial or regional authorities. Nor should one overlook research workers or specialists who are capable of carrying out theoretical or applied studies. But since the success of an innovation depends, in the last analysis, on the attitude of teachers and organizers it will, above all, be necessary to make all possible arrangements to relay information to the schools and to bodies dealing with adult education. Only at this price will a system of international exchange become truly effective.

Studies

Since research work and in-depth studies with a view to the selection of innovations must be carried out in each individual country, the aim of international co-operation should be to help national establishments to accomplish this demanding task. In this, too, the IBE has a central role to play, by launching a large-scale programme of studies : initially, case studies, of the kind which OECD has been successfully publishing for many years, but which would apply exclusively to innovations of particular interest. Starting from a set of cases, some comparative studies would attempt to detect likenesses and differences in the innovations themselves, and others would aim to throw into relief the common features and similarities of the necessary conditions. This should make it possible to clarify individual factors in this cluster of problems surrounding innovations, which the International Commission on the Development of Education was able to do no more than outline, and to frame an idea of the typology which it did not have time to consider in detail. If, at an early date, the national authorities and their educational research centres can count on the invaluable aid of problem-analysis and typology, international co-operation will have fulfilled the wishes of the Commission by establishing throughout the world a genuine 'network of change'.

Technical assistance

In a field where grey matter is of vital importance, co-operation
among nations might be confined to that intellectual exchange
service which the IBE is fully capable of providing. However, the
International Conference on Education foresaw that technical assistance would be indispensable. Once decisions have been taken in
each of the States concerned, many of them will still need international assistance for the implementation of the strategies which
they have framed. There will then be a transition from intellectual
co-operation to operational action, which will depend either on
bilateral aid, according to agreements concluded between individual States, or on aid from the United Nations system and, in
particular, Unesco. In fact, these two forms of aid have long been
encouraging large-scale innovations, such as functional literacy
training, the launching of educational television in the Ivory Coast
and India's use of an artificial satellite for adult education. On a
smaller scale, with the financial assistance of the United Nations
Development Programme, the World Bank or the United Nations
Children's Fund, Unesco grants direct aid to many developing
countries for educational renovation, teacher training, the development of educational research or educational planning. It is surely
true to say that all these activities already tend to foster a spirit
of innovation.

The strength of a programme devoted solely to innovations
would lie in its ability to give rise to new strategies, to encourage
a search for alternatives to what already exists, and especially to
protect the developing countries from the temptation to adopt
models imported from the most highly-developed countries. It
remains to be seen what forms of help a judiciously chosen kind
of technical assistance will be able to offer the Third World.
Immediately upon entering the vast field of technical assistance,
one is suddenly faced with all the questions raised by international
action with a view to economic and social development. The
implications of these questions are far too broad and complex
to be dealt with in this study. But since the answers to them affect
the future of international aid to education, we cannot afford to
pass them over in silence, if only for the sake of measuring the
gravity and urgency of the problem.

Editorial note. Since Mr. Jean Thomas wrote this section on 'An international programme for innovation' a new Unesco programme has been started at the International Bureau of Education (Geneva) under the title 'International Educational Reporting Service' (IERS).

The principal aim of the service is to provide information about innovations which have a high relevance to developing countries. It will be designed to serve educational leaders in such countries, particularly those who decide policies and plan and administer education systems, so that they may be aware of the various possibilities open to them. Thus the IERS is seen as one instrument for helping in the renovation of national systems of education. It follows that the reports issued by the service will deal with subject areas of priority concern to developing countries. The emphasis lies on case materials about new ways of organizing the teaching and learning process which appear to lead to improved and wider educational opportunities without undue cost.

Although the IERS is placed in the IBE, it is taking shape as a network programme rather than a centralized operation. The Unesco Regional Offices for Education and the field programmes of Unesco as well as of Unicef, ILO and FAO are associated as partners in the service. Still more important, national institutions for educational information and research will be involved, to carry out studies and to supply and use the information, so that the network for exchange of innovatory experiences will be a reality.

The IERS programme has been made possible through voluntary financial contributions from a number of international and bilateral agencies and national institutions. The seven donors at present are Unicef, the aid agencies of Canada, Sweden, United Kingdom, United States, the International Development Research Centre (Ottawa) and the Ford Foundation.

Chapter seven

A crisis in international co-operation?

It will be remembered that, in the last chapter of its report, the International Commission on the Development of Education observed that co-operation in education was in the throes of a crisis similar to that currently affecting all international aid to development. Recalling, without openly endorsing, the most common broadsides of criticism fired at international co-operation, the Commission specifically mentions inadequacy of voluntary contributions, political or commercial advantages which donor States hope to reap from their assistance, wastage of resources and practical ineffectiveness of means and the deplorable habit of offering foreign models to the developing countries when these do not correspond to their true needs. [1]

In his full and meaty introduction to the report on the activities of Unesco in 1973, the Director-General, Mr. René Maheu, does not use the word 'crisis', but he nevertheless points out the weaknesses and shortcomings of co-operation for development : his discussions with governments and his visits to projects being carried out in the field convinced him more and more each day 'of the need to carry out a thorough review of the aid provided ... through the United Nations system ... as regards alike the aims pursued, the methods followed and the machinery employed' [5, p. xxix]. The Commission talks of a crisis, and one of the most senior international civil servants testifies to a need for radical change : both views sound alarming. Our comments should no doubt be confined

1. See, *Learning to be* [9] Chapter 9, entitled 'Roads to solidarity'.

to the educational field, but nowadays it would be unrealistic to separate education from other factors of development. To call international aid to development in question is at the same time to subject all the objectives, methods and procedures of international aid to education to a careful scrutiny.

INTELLECTUAL CO-OPERATION

Because education nowadays raises problems which extend beyond the control of even the most advanced countries, taken individually, the report of the Edgar Faure Commission submits that international exchanges of information, experience and individuals are more than ever necessary. And, true enough, the machinery of intellectual co-operation is patently gaining in strength and sophistication. But contrary to popular belief, this form of co-operation is not based on age-old tradition. While it is true that thinkers, scholars and theorists have always, throughout the world, and especially throughout Europe, formed a genuine intellectual community, linked together by the publication of their work and by active private correspondence, it was not until the beginning of this century that the decision was taken to set up a permanent body specifically for education. Until after the Second World War, the International Bureau of Education, founded in Geneva, was the only establishment of its kind. Even in the League of Nations, despite the fact that it had planned from the outset to set up a Commission to examine international matters of intellectual co-operation and education, the opinion prevailed for a long time that education, considered as a prerogative of the authorities of each State, was outside the field of competence of an international organization. It was remarkable that the Commission, once established, and the [International] Institute of Intellectual Co-operation, placed at the disposal of the League of Nations by France, were able to go so far as to raise certain problems of higher education and to seek the support of the universities, much more for the sake of science than for that of education. [1] Eventually

1. On this matter see *The International Institute of Intellectual Co-operation,* published by the Institute in Paris in 1946.

Unesco made its appearance, and education was officially recognized as one of the fundamental fields of co-operation among States.

International and regional co-operation

This time, however, it was given pride of place. We have come a long way in a little more than twenty years. The present structures of Unesco speak for themselves. At the top, the General Conference, attended every two years by the delegations of the Member States which are usually headed by Ministers of Education, is responsible mainly for the adoption of the Organization's programmes, in which the highest priority has so far been given to projects connected with education. During the year when the General Conference does not meet, a session of the International Conference on Education is held in Geneva : its agenda includes, as we have seen, an assessment of recent progress and a study in depth of one of the more urgent issues confronting all States. The educational authorities of each country are thus able to keep abreast of new and important current of forthcoming events in the other countries of the world.

Unesco is now able to call upon three specialized bodies to help in this task. In Geneva, the IBE, for documentation, dissemination of information and studies ; in Hamburg, the Unesco Institute for Education, which deals chiefly with research ; in Paris, the International Institute for Educational Planning, which is concerned both with research and with the further training of highly qualified personnel.

This powerful international machinery is matched, at the level of each of the major geographical or cultural regions, by a network of co-operative bodies. Ministers of Education in the same region meet at regular intervals to compare notes, to chart progress and to evaluate the needs of their countries. Unesco Offices for Education are established in the four principal regions : in Dakar for Africa, in Santiago for Latin America and the Caribbean, in Beirut for the Arab States and in Bangkok for Asia. Their duties include studies and surveys with a view to analysing the situation and trends of education in the Member States of the region, the collection and dissemination of information and documentation in collaboration with the IBE, and the training and further training of educational planners and teaching personnel as well as the architects and engineers assigned to the task of building school premises.

The United Nations University

At university level, where teaching is combined with research, Unesco also maintains regional offices for scientific co-operation, such as those in Nairobi for Africa, Montevideo for Latin America, Cairo for the Arab States, New Delhi for South Asia and Djakarta for South East Asia.

The most outstanding achievement in this field was undoubtedly the establishment of an international university in 1972. This had already been proposed to the United Nations General Assembly by its Secretary-General in 1969 and, in the years that followed, the foundation of this new institution was a focus of close collaboration between the United Nations and Unesco. A Founding Committee, appointed by the Secretary-General in consultation with the Director-General of Unesco, had already held two meetings by the end of 1973, and on the basis of its report the supreme authorities of the two organizations adopted the Charter of the 'United Nations University'. It was decided that the latter should take the form of a network of research and training institutions for postgraduate students. Fields of study were centred on subjects of world-wide relevance, requiring the collaboration of research workers drawn from a variety of disciplines and regions. According to this plan, the purpose of the United Nations University will therefore be to give worldwide encouragement and support to existing universities and research centres wishing to improve or modernize their programmes, and to add a universal dimension to their outlook. To disseminate knowledge, foster exchanges of individuals in the academic world and encourage the growth of fruitful ideas : this should be the principal role of the new university. It will therefore enjoy total autonomy, and its Charter provides for its complete freedom of action. Its budget will be financed by voluntary contributions.

At the generous invitation of the Japanese Government, the central bodies of the university—Council, Rector and administrative departments—will be housed in Tokyo, but the institutions called upon to participate in its work must be scattered throughout all the regions of the world, and the only criterion for their participation must be that of the quality and effectiveness of their contributions. As for the programmes, the resolution adopted by the United Nations General Assembly assigns to the Council the task of drawing them up, with the sole proviso that they should be devoted to 'action-oriented research into the pressing global problems of human survival, development and welfare'. It has, moreover, been agreed that the work of the university will also assist the international organizations of the United Nations system in clarifying and improving their own programmes, and will help to train national experts for Member States, as well as international experts. Although it is not yet possible to foresee the practical form which the university's activities, or even its disciplines, will take, one can here and now hail the foundation of the United Nations University as the supreme expression of intellectual co-operation.

OPERATIONAL AID TO EDUCATION

Intellectual co-operation has long been recognized as essential to the acquisition and dissemination of knowledge, as well as to the progress of research in the various intellectual disciplines. In the past few years, it has therefore become a powerful stimulus to the universal development of education. This form of international co-operation is showing no signs of a crisis ; on the contrary, it is going from strength to strength, to the satisfaction of all concerned. It was not this co-operation that the Edgar Faure Commission was calling in question ; nor was it to this that the Director-General of Unesco was referring when he said that it should be subjected to radical revision. Insofar as the crisis exists, it can affect only operational forms of international aid to education, i.e. those which consist in helping the States of the Third World to devise, plan or carry out, in their own countries, projects designed to accelerate their development.

Bilateral and multilateral aid

The various types of aid to education have two different sources : the first, known as bilateral aid, consists in the implementation of agreements concluded directly between States ; the second, known as multilateral, stems from the execution of programmes drawn up by the international organizations of the United Nations system. The objectives of aid, whether bilateral or multilateral, are always the same, as are its procedures ; and it is always voluntary. Moreover the same countries are always parties to it. Only their motives are different. Bilateral aid is often criticized for not springing from disinterested motives. In giving multilateral aid, the donor States merge into collective anonymity, but in concluding agreements with the States of their choice, they preserve their identity and their distinctive image. They undoubtedly hope to maintain privileged relations with the recipient countries ; political ulterior motives are seldom absent. Sometimes the agreements even contain clauses promising favourable conditions for the industry or trade of the State which grants 'tied aid'. So it is easy to understand that the Edgar Faure Commission should have severely condemned a practice which strays so far from the ideal of international solidarity [9, p. 254]. But how can one overlook the fact that public opinion, which is often reluctant to make financial sacrifices, considers the national interest to be a decisive argument ? Even if the reasons behind it are not as pure as might be hoped, it is not a trivial matter if aid to development finally wins the day. Nor, in the name of international solidarity, can one condemn the bonds which link former metropolitan countries to their former colonies. If the United Kingdom and France feel particularly responsible for the fate of certain countries which have gained their independence in Africa, in Asia or off the coast of America, this is surely due to a historically determined type of solidarity, and to the implicit desire to redress the injustices of the past. It is not difficult to find sound reasons for such choices.

The Scandinavian States, which do not have the same worries, afford an example worth noting. For many years they have preferred multilateral co-operation, to which they contribute very generously, but they nevertheless take a more active interest in certain chosen fields such as adult education or vocational training.

Hence an original form of aid which might well be called 'multi-bilateral', reflecting both its collective nature and the areas of priority to which it is directed. [1]

Whatever its underlying motives, it can scarcely be denied that bilateral aid is more rapid and less expensive than multilateral assistance. One need only refer back to the report of the Director-General of Unesco in order to take stock of the slowness and inflexibility of international procedures, and the 'costly commitments' which they impose on countries receiving aid, not to mention the competition and even rivalry to which they give rise between the specialized agencies participating in them. So true is this that, if one weighs the advantages and disadvantages of the two forms of aid, there seems little to choose between them. The only conclusion to be drawn from this long-standing debate is that they are both necessary, and that, instead of conflicting, they should complement each other. The principle of country programming, which makes the recipient State the sole judge, has fortunately put an end to a conflict which is both absurd and sterile. From now on it is the responsibility of the government of the country concerned to make a final assessment of all the forms and procedures of assistance which it finds useful, and to co-ordinate the different types of operational action to its advantage, irrespective of their origin.

Volume of international aid to education

It is not easy to evaluate precisely the global volume of international aid chanelled into education, or to compare the total funds provided by bilateral aid with those arising from multilateral aid. The figures are not reliable and the dates do not coincide. Only approximate estimates are therefore possible. According to the report of the Edgar Faure Commission, which was based on OECD data and on the calculations of certains experts, it was estimated that public or private bilateral aid to education, for the year 1970-1971, amounted to a total somewhere between $US1,660 and

1. In this connexion see the article by Lars Olof Edström, 'A Scandinavian perspective on aid to education', in the summer 1974 issue of the review *Prospects* [17].

1,760 million. The total amount of multilateral aid provided to education in the framework of the United Nations and through Unesco was $US281,219,000 in 1973. Even if the difference in the dates is taken into account, one can safely conclude that the amount spent on bilateral aid, in 1972 or thereabouts, was approximately six times greater than that spent on multilateral aid. If one adds the two figures, one arrives at a total of nearly $US2,000 million for international aid to education as a whole.

This figure, probably inaccurate, is not enough by itself to convey a clear idea of the effort made ; no sound argument could be based on it except by comparing it with that of over-all spending on education by the various States. But here, too, the statistics are incomplete. [1] The Edgar Faure Commission was on shaky ground when it drew the conclusion that aid granted in 1968 represented approximately 10 per cent of the educational expenses of the developing countries. A slightly more recent estimate [15] raises this figure up to 12 per cent. This, again, is only an average, since aid is unequally distributed and rises as high as 30 or 40 per cent in the more advantaged countries.

It is true that aid proper supplements the loans granted by certain States and by international bodies such as the World Bank ($US425 million in June 1971), the Inter-American Development Bank (slightly more than $US150 million at the end of the same year) or the European Development Fund ($US145 million at the end of 1969). But with a few rare exceptions, the rates of interest are a fairly heavy burden for the recipient countries : the rate of the World Bank was 7 per cent in 1970.

What conclusion is to be drawn from all these figures ? International aid to education, whether in the form of technical assistance or of investment funds, is certainly not something to be brushed aside ; nor is it brushed aside. The countries of the Third World receive it with great enthusiasm, and it has already enabled them to carry out a great many useful projects in setting up establishments for higher, secondary or technical education, training qualified personnel, equipping laboratories and libraries and strengthening the fight against illiteracy. It also encourages them

1. The figures for several States, including China, are not available. In this connexion, see *Learning to be* [9], Table 13 on page 288.

to adopt more reliable methods in planning educational development and improving administrative procedures. To deny the importance of these projects would be to deny the obvious. But it is nonetheless certain that this type of aid is still very inadequate ; it is poorly distributed, it benefits chiefly those countries which are the least disadvantaged, and it provokes at least as much criticism as praise. Is there any hope that, in the years to come, there will be a massive increase in international aid to education ? The tendency seems to be towards a decrease. A reduction has already been observed in the share of their national income which the donor States set aside for technical or financial assistance to development ; economic circumstances, austerity policies and credit restrictions are all discouraging signs. The only grounds for hope seem to be the rapid enrichment of countries which supply raw materials as necessary and as invaluable as oil. If these countries agree to be generous and to supply aid not only to those States which suit their political preferences but also to those which stand in most urgent need of it, then perhaps a small ray of light may pierce the gloom ahead.

Psychological difficulties

The difficulties encountered by international co-operation in its operational aspects have other causes apart from financial ones. Psychological problems account for a good deal. One of the most common types of aid, in the form of bilateral action and action by international bodies, consists of fellowship programmes for training or further training abroad. Countless young graduates of Third World universities dream of going to complete their education in one of the centres famous throughout the world for the advanced specialized training in science or technology which they provide. And there can be few governments of poor countries short of qualified personnel which have not thought of taking advantage of these attractive prospects. But the disappointments are also innumerable. The brain drain, as the Americans call it, is too well-known a phenomenon to need enlarging upon. The lure of high salaries, extremely favourable living and working conditions, opportunities for rapid advancement and a career in laboratories, firms or research establishments—no other reasons are needed, surely, to explain the number of young scientists or technicians who abandon the idea of returning to their country of origin [19]. There are also phenomena of a psychological nature, to which little study has so far been devoted, namely : 'drain within each underdeveloped society, i.e. the estrangement of the intellectual from the society in which he lives, his isolation, which ... has more serious consequences than drain abroad.' [1] So, for some years now, an effort has been made to curtail training programmes abroad and especially to monitor them more effectively. An attempt is being made to avoid sending abroad students who are too young or insufficiently mature, and educational and training facilities are provided for them at home instead ; on their return, an effort is made to ensure that they will find jobs which are better suited to their skills. But the risks are still high, and a solution has by no means been found to this serious problem.

Psychologists could also say a great deal about the difficulties encountered or created by experts sent to developing countries. As we know, experts serve a dual purpose : firstly, they must place their experience at the disposal of the governments or establishments of the country to which they are assigned, and, secondly, they must provide expert training for nationals of that country who are destined to replace them at a later date. But, however great the skill or devotion of each of these foreign experts, their very position arouses the most lively and varied criticism. They are reproached with not knowing the people among whom they are called upon to live, being unable to adapt to their customs, beliefs or culture, and holding themselves aloof from local society like an irredeemably foreign body. This occurs to such an extent that, on hearing the reproaches so often hurled at them, somebody once remarked that, in order to be a good expert in a developing country one would have to be both a hero and a saint.

In this case, as in the case of fellowship for training abroad, the bodies responsible for aid are leaving no stone unturned in their search for remedies. Much greater care is being taken in recruiting experts and, before being sent out, they are given the

---

1. These lines and several of the remarks which follow have been taken from a penetrating study by Juan Gomez Millas, 'The development ethic', published in the summer 1974 issue of *Prospects* [17].

most reliable information possible on their countries of assignment
and on the peoples among whom they are going to live ; pains
are also taken to assess their adaptability to new conditions. But
experts are like teachers : competence is not enough, a flair for
teaching is also required, as well as a feeling for human relations,
and these qualities will come out only in their work. The stigma
he bears as a foreigner will follow the expert everywhere and
whatever he does ; it may give him greater prestige, but it will also
create great difficulties for him. This is what an acute observer has
to say on the subject :

> 'The foreign experts who in an initial phase may be perfectly
> well-equipped for clarifying the future tasks of a society beget
> experts from the assisted society who are often more able
> to understand the workings of their own country than
> foreigners can. It is then that a rivalry develops between
> foreign and national experts, at which point the institutions
> dispensing the aid need to revise their roles for the appoint-
> ment of staff and, so far as possible, use local personnel in
> planning and development programmes. Many specialists
> believe that a positive effect may be obtained if we recall that
> almost every developing country has a modernized sector to
> some extent which can be used to adapt technologies.' [1]

These comments are particularly apposite in the case of education
as a whole. Specialists, certainly competent but insufficiently
informed about local conditions are sometimes brought from afar
and at great expense, despite the fact that local personnel, in
a university or a research or training centre, might more usefully
be drawn on. It should be a golden rule of international co-
operation that national resources must be developed to the full.

Furthermore, wherever he comes from, a foreign expert necessarily brings with him certain concepts, habits or experience, which
have the greatest difficulty in taking root in new ground. How can
a teaching method be truly endogenous, as is frequently recommended, if its only support comes from foreign advisers ? How
can an innovation blend in with the national system if it is introduced from outside ?

---

1. See the article by Jean Gomez Millas, *op. cit.*

Not only the origin of experts, but also their function and their point of impact should be reviewed. Recourse to foreign advisers is effective only if they can be fitted into the heart of the system, the central organ on which everything else depends. The disordered proliferation of experts should be abandoned and fewer experts assigned to missions which have been carefully thought out.

Mistakes in diagnosis

This brings us to problems of another kind. A close examination of programmes of aid to education drawn up so far, reveals a surprising diversity and dispersion of effort. Initially, what was obviously required was action to deal with an emergency situation. Everything needed to be done, and every aspect of the problem was indeed tackled at the same time : illiteracy, primary education, secondary education, technical education, higher education, adult education, teacher training, educational documentation, teaching methods, textbooks, audio-visual aids and school buildings. This many-pronged attack was justified, and in each case experts had to be recruited, solutions suggested and models proposed. But where were these experts and models to be found if not in the large metropolitan countries of the West ? Thus under pressure of circumstances rather than in accordance with a premeditated design, the Third World countries adopted the educational objectives, customs and methods of the far-off countries which offered them assistance.

Now that the time has come to take stock, it is easier to evaluate the mistakes in diagnosis made and the poor results achieved. Yet there is no question of a blanket condemnation of this proliferation of clumsy experiments. Millions of illiterates were made literate, millions of children were enrolled at school, large numbers of teachers are being turned out by training centres, and universities have sprung up in the most remote areas. But it is also evident that this type of education is ill-suited to the needs, structures and aspirations of society in these countries, and that it does not correspond to the culture of their peoples. But then throughout this study we have been coming across these symptoms of a dangerous unsuitability and the effects of alienation.

As the conditions necessary for development became more clearly apparent, other errors of diagnosis were identified. Praiseworthy efforts have certainly been made to plan educational resources as part of a much broader development plan. Yet, just as the education systems proposed to the Third World originated in the Western and former metropolitan countries, so development became patterned on the most industrialized societies. Rapid industrialization and industry-oriented education were initially the objectives to which top priority was accorded. These objectives are certainly still valid for a certain number of countries which have already advanced further than others along the path of development. Nevertheless, the vast majority of Third World countries now admit bitterly how wrong they were to neglect the needs of their agriculture and the welfare of their rural population. There is at present general recognition of the fact that a sharp change of direction is necessary, as regards not only the training of young people who have been to school as well as those who have not, but also the course to be steered for the economy as a whole. None of the international or regional conferences held in recent years has failed to come to the conclusion that it is vitally necessary to give the highest priority to education in rural areas.

THE ROLE OF EDUCATION IN DEVELOPMENT

None of these problems was overlooked by the International Commission on the Development of Education. Certain perspicacious readers may feel disappointed by the shortcomings and uncertainties which they feel are to be found in its report, but this is because there are still shortcomings and obscurities in the relationship between development and education and even in the very idea of development itself. Yet it is clear that ideas have evolved considerably. During the initial period, corresponding to the nineteen-sixties, people were rather too ready to believe that education by itself was going to give the nations of the Third World sufficient impetus to embark on the path of autonomous development.

At the end of this first development decade, the fact had to be faced that this hope had not been fulfilled. The conclusion drawn was that education should participate in other development activities. For example, we have already seen how far training was dependent on employment and how agricultural development called for over-all strategies involving close co-ordination of education, employment, investment and trade policies.

By 1969, the report of the Commission on International Development, usually called after its principal author, Lester B. Pearson, had revealed new development prospects. Since then, ideas have changed still further, to such an extent that the advent of a new world economic order is considered possible. The time seems ripe to subject the problems and procedures of development to a more ambitious investigation, better adapted to present-day circumstances. One may even wonder whether it would not have been preferable to do this at the outset, before appointing an international commission to map out the future of education in the context of future economic and social development. International bodies do not always proceed in a logical order.

An over-all development strategy

There is an increasing trend towards an over-all conception of development and towards measures to provide technical or financial aid based on strategies—also comprehensive—in which education will have its rightful place, since no project must henceforth be approved by the higher authorities if it does not include training activities. This is certainly a realistic attitude, worthy of approval, but it implies profound changes in the objectives, procedures and actual circumstances of international co-operation. The body responsible for programming is still, and must remain, the government of the recipient State : it alone is responsible for drawing up its development plan, framing its policy and adopting its strategies in the light of its own resources and the foreign aid which it hopes to receive. It is therefore that government's responsibility to co-ordinate and guide the action taken by its various ministries, its specialized administrative departments and all national institutions—including those dealing with education—at all levels. But as it is to be anticipated that this task, which calls for both over-all vision and technical skill, will appear too demanding to the governments of many developing countries, which have neither the requisite structures nor personnel, they can be expected to ask for assistance and advice from foreign experts, no longer on an emergency basis, but for the development of entire patterns of decisions on policies, strategies and development planning. How are such experts to be selected, where should they be recruited and what tasks should be assigned to them so as to avoid a repetition of past errors ? How far can foreign advisers co-operate in genuinely national development or, as it is commonly called nowadays, 'endogenous' development ? The problem of experts still remains to be solved.

Problems of co-ordination

The other major difficulty stems from the lack of co-ordination among the international agencies concerned with development, and even in the education sector alone. According to an expert in these matters :

'Education and training are of some concern in one way or another in most of the fourteen Specialized Agencies and eight semi-autonomous units of the United Nations system. While Unesco's primacy in the field of education is widely recognized, governments may also consult : ILO for advice concerning vocational training, FAO with regard to the professional preparation of farmers and agricultural specialists ; WHO in connexion with the education and training of professional, technical and auxiliary staff for health services ; the World Bank group for capital aid to education ; Unicef to help children who are educationally deprived—to name only a few of the educational activities covered by other United Nations Agencies.'[1]

It is true that these agencies have concluded agreements among themselves in order to delimit their respective fields of competence and facilitate their co-operation. It is also true that the heads of agencies meet at regular intervals in a committee on co-ordination, and that the United Nations Economic and Social Council is officially responsible for receiving their reports and laying down common guidelines for them. The problems of employment and

1. See the article by William J. Platt in the summer 1974 issue of *Prospects*, p. 249 [17].

their impact on vocational training have become much more widely known since the ILO's World Programme made provision for joint missions to various countries to study over-all employment strategies. Due weight is also attached to the meetings organized privately by the Ford Foundation and the Rockefeller Foundation to foster exchanges of views and projects between directors of major international institutions and educators or statesmen from Third World countries. The need for greater coherence is now obvious to everyone, and high hopes are in order. But it is also understandable that a cumbersome and complex machine of this kind moves slowly, that it requires negotiations at every level, and that technical hitches sometimes occur. The road to integrated development remains strewn with obstacles.

Political options

It is impossible to talk of these institutional difficulties without going on to mention the problems connected with the political options of individual Third World countries. In the first phase, which was one of inexperience and grand illusions, attention was focused chiefly on the purely economic features of development, such as the growth of the national product varying in extent and rapidly from case to case. But more inquiring minds were not slow to feel concern about the sharing out of material benefits among the various segments of society. The social and human aspects of development should, in their view, take priority over the directly measurable effects of expansion. Still more recently, reliable observers raised the question how the transformations imposed by the importation of modern technologies were going to affect the customs, thought patterns and beliefs of the developing peoples, and what kinds of distortion, tension, or disruption might threaten their mental balance. And as the serious question of the preservation of their cultural identity was raised at the same time, problems of development, already so complex, took on a new, cultural dimension.

It would certainly be unreasonable to consider in the same way, and to treat as a homogeneous group, countries which differ so much in size, population and economic structure, as Brazil, Mexico, and India on the one hand, and many small African or

Caribbean States on the other, which might seem unlikely at present to be able to stand on their own feet, economically speaking. There are many degrees of under-development. But even in those developing countries where expansion has been most rapid and most spectacular, wide discrepancies are to be observed in the circumstances of various social categories. Development has primarily benefited certain sectors of activity and ways of thought which are in every way similar to those of their Western counterparts, whereas the rest of the population, particularly farmers or craft-workers, have lingered on in the same conditions of poverty and insecurity that prevailed before the beginning of economic growth. Without realizing it, or at least without admitting it, the leaders of these countries seem to have opted for such inequality. Perhaps they think that prosperity will be contagious and will gradually spread to the whole population, the privileged sectors inevitably drawing the others after them.

However, other Third World countries, following China's example, have opted for slower but more uniform development—for progress which is less spectacular but more evenly distributed. They appeal primarily to the principle of justice : justice among nations and, within a single nation, among all categories of people ; justice which is both economic, through the establishment of a new world order, and social, in a revolutionary context. [1]

This choice of a blueprint for society is, of course, reflected in the educational projects and cultural policies of individual countries. In some cases, reform of the education system will aim above all at better adaptation and more satisfactory training of young people and adults, whereas others will not hesitate to plunge into radical transformation and make very bold innovations. It is no accident that the Cuban or Peruvian experiments follow that of China in this second category of reforms. They are truly revolutionary reforms, in keeping with the ideologies that these countries uphold. It is only natural that the objectives and methods of international aid should be affected by them, and the harmony of international assemblies disturbed. In the name of this new

1. A rough analysis of these situations is to be found in the summer 1974 issue of the review *Prospects*, in the article by Tibor Mende, 'Aid in its context' (p. 198-204) [17].

concept of development, the established order of inter-State relations is now being challenged, both in education and in the economic sphere.

Problems peculiar to education

Education nevertheless continues to raise problems of its own which should not be overlooked simply because an over-all approach to development aid is adopted. A tendency is emerging among the staunchest supporters of integrated strategies to talk more readily about *training* than about *education*. The reason is no doubt that training, being a direct preparation for vocational activity, is more easily slotted into a single over-all project. But if teaching, out-of-school education and adult education are chopped up like this into operational chunks according to the needs of the moment, there is surely a risk of losing sight of that broad, comprehensive outlook which must guide the future of education. Urged to adopt this new approach to development, how can governments succeed in working out over-all educational projects and how can the international authorities organize over-all aid to education, if education is once again split up into a mass of fragmented activities and if development strategies are not attuned to education strategies ? Will the progress so dearly bought on one count be cancelled out on another ?

The trouble with education is that it is always torn between conflicting requirements. Insofar as it is regarded as a necessary factor of development, it must certainly be treated as one means among many, on a par with health, labour, employment, agriculture, trade or industry. But if its acknowledged purpose is to shape a complete human being who is 'learning to be', then education becomes the highest ambition of every individual, of every society and of mankind as a whole. It is no longer a means but an end. How can these two requirements be reconciled, and how can international co-operation take them into account without sacrificing either ?

The answer is quite obvious. In operational action, a distinction must be drawn between projects which relate chiefly to over-all aid to development and those which aim rather at promoting education. In the first case, training programmes will form an essential part of all projects, according to an integrated approach. But in the second, action should be taken at the most suitable junctures in order to bring about an effective change in the education systems as a whole, and it is at those points that well-planned innovations can have the most telling effect. To put an end to the proliferation of limited short-term interventions, to concentrate efforts on a small number of efficient projects and to build up promising strategies : this should be the chief concern of the national authorities responsible for programming aid, and also that of the international bodies whose business it is to implement the programmes.

On the other hand, single-minded intellectual co-operation in the interest of over-all aid to education will continue. Indeed, regular exchanges of information and experience, and periodical meetings between authorities and experts are the surest means of achieving the adaptation and renovation of the entire education fabric. And such meetings and exchanges will also provide operational action with the conceptual basis—the infrastructure of thought and study—that it so badly needs. In all matters connected with education, whether it be considered as a means or as an end, both forms of co-operation, intellectual and operational, must be closely united and complementary. But the fact must be acknowledged that such solidarity and complementarity have not yet been achieved ; far from it.

THE FUTURE OF INTERNATIONAL CO-OPERATION

Does this analysis prompt the conclusion that international co-operation is in the throes of a crisis or that aid to education is in danger ? If we can only call a brief halt to complaints about the quantitative inadequacy of international assistance (without necessarily abandoning the idea of exploring avenues still open to a better tomorrow), we are led to measure the gravity or urgency of problems, rather than to contemplate the future with dread. Nobody disputes the fact that errors have been made, that illusions have been shattered, that there have been wrong diagnoses and erroneous courses of treatment, and that many efforts have been in vain. But the lessons of the past are not wasted. The international agencies have learnt to co-ordinate their activities more satisfactorily by overcoming their foolish rivalries. The day is perhaps not far off when they will be able to make their machinery more flexible and speed up their action. The research everywhere being carried out has already shed some light on the phenomenon of development and has greatly illuminated the needs of education. The world has never had at its disposal so many tools with which to combat the threats of poverty, ignorance and hunger. The path of solidarity, straight and broad, lies ahead of mankind.

But this path is still strewn with obstacles. Why, in international assemblies where the most pressing problems are discussed and where plans for co-operation are drawn up, must the harsh claims of some provoke the bitterness of others, to no purpose ? The more urgent the need for solidarity, the more one may observe partisan passions dividing States into hostile groups. No doubt, as much at international level as in each society, the voice of justice is not soothing ; progress cannot be achieved without a struggle. But since all States join specialized agencies with the firm intention of working together on common tasks of major importance then, surely, reason, if not emotion, should impel them to seek for that which unites them rather than to persist in emphasizing what divides them. If a crisis should threaten international co-operation or weaken aid to education, the cause will not lie in the difficulty of selecting more reasonable objectives or more efficient methods. The cause will be the distaste which States seem to feel for proceeding together along the path of solidarity.

Select bibliography

This bibliography contains only the principal sources of documentation used during the writing of this study, as well as a few publications, books and articles which the reader might find useful.

A. Unesco official documents

1. Regional Conference of Ministers of Education and those responsible for Economic Planning in Asia, 3rd, Singapore, 31 May–7 June 1971. *Final report.* Paris, Unesco, 1971. 91 p. (ED/MD/20.)

2. Conference of Ministers of Education and those responsible for the Promotion of Science and Technology in relation to Development in Latin America and the Caribbean, Venezuela, 6-15 December 1971. *Final report.* Paris, Unesco, 1972. (ED/MD/22.)

3. Third International Conference on Adult Education:
    (a) International Conference on Adult Education, 3rd, Tokyo, 25 July–7 August 1972. *A retrospective international survey of adult education (Montreal 1960 to Tokyo 1972).* Paris, Unesco, 1972. 135 p. (Unesco/CONFEDAD/4.)
    (b) ——. *Adult education in the context of lifelong education.* Paris, Unesco, 1972. 34 p. (Unesco/CONFEDAD/5.)
    (c) ——. *Final report.* Paris, Unesco, 1972. 101 p. (ED/MD/25.)

4. International Conference on Education, 34th Session:
    (a) International Conference on Education, 34th Session, Geneva, 19-27 September 1973. *The relationship between education, training and employment, with particular reference to secondary education, its aims, structure and content.* Paris, Unesco, 1973. 65 p. (ED/BIE/CONFINTED 34/5.)
    (b) ——. *Main trends in education.* Paris, Unesco, 1973. 19 p. (ED/BIE/CONFINTED 34/4.)
    (c) ——. *A summary statistical review of education in the world of the sixties.* Paris, Unesco, 1973. 38 p. (ED/BIE/CONFINTED 34/Ref. 1.)

(d) ——. *Education for rural life with particular reference to the secondary level*, by Jean Jacques Deheyn and John Higgs. Paris, Unesco, 1973. 16 p. (ED/BIE/CONFINTED 34/Ref. 2.)

(e) ——. *Education, the labour market and employment*, by Jean Versluis. Paris, Unesco, 1973. 11 p. (ED/BIE/CONFINTED 34/Ref. 4.)

(f) ——. *Criteria and mechanisms of evaluation in secondary education*; summary of an international study, by A.M. Huberman and J. Stroumza. Paris, Unesco, 1973. 14 p. in various pagings. (ED/BIE/CONFINTED 34/Ref. 5.)

(g) ——. *Young people's attitudes to school, the adult world and employment*; a digest of an international survey, by Pierre Dominicé. Paris, Unesco, 1973. 10 p. (ED/BIE/CONFINTED 34/Ref. 6.)

(h) ——. *Ongoing social education*; paper prepared by a group of non-governmental organizations. Paris, Unesco, 1973. 9 p. (ED/BIE/CONFINTED 34/Ref. 7.)

(i) ——. *Final report*. Paris, Unesco, 1973. 64 p. (ED/MD/29.)

5. General Conference, Eighteenth Session, Paris, 1974. *Report of the Director-General on the activities of the organization in 1973*. Paris, Unesco, 1974. 306 p.

6. Second Conference of Ministers of Education of European Member States:

(a) Conference of Ministers of Education of European Member States, 2nd, Bucharest, 26 November–4 December 1973. *Higher education in Europe: problems and prospects*. Paris, Unesco, 1973. 74 p. in various pagings. (ED-73/MINEUROP II/3.)

(b) ——. *Higher education in Europe: problems and prospects; statistical study*. Paris, Unesco, 1973. 49 p.; 40 p., appendix. (ED-73/MINEUROP II/Ref. 1.)

(c) ——. *Final report*. Paris, Unesco, 1974. 79 p. (ED/MD/30.)

B. Other publications of Unesco

7. Dave, R.H. *Lifelong education and school curriculum: interim findings of an exploratory study on school curriculum, structures and teacher education in the perspective of lifelong education*. Hamburg, Unesco, Institute for Education, 1973. 90 p. (UIE monographs, 1.)

8. ——; Stiemerling, N., eds. *Lifelong education and the school: abstracts and bibliography/ L'éducation permanente et l'école: extraits et bibliographie*. Hamburg, Unesco Institute for Education, 1973. 154 p. (UIE monographs, 2.)

9. Faure, E., et al. *Learning to be: the world of education today and tomorrow*. Paris, Unesco; London, Harrap, 1972. 313 p. [Appendix 5 of the Report gives a list of the many documents prepared for the International Commission on the Development of Education. These documents can be consulted at Unesco.]

10. Hely, A.S.M. *New trends in adult education: from Elsinore to Montreal*. Paris, Unesco, 1962. 136 p. (Monographs on education, IV.)

11. International Institute for Educational Planning. *Educational costs and productivity.* Contribution to a seminar for professors of educational planning (economics) of the regional centres of Unesco, held at the International Institute for Educational Planning, 5-16 June 1967. Paris, Unesco: International Institute for Educational Planning, 1973. 1 vol., various pagings.

12. Lallez, R. *The TEVEC case: an experiment in adult education using the multi-media system.* Paris, Unesco: IBE, 1973. 64 p. (Experiments and innovations in education, no. 1.)

13. Lengrand, P. *An introduction to lifelong education.* Paris, Unesco, 1970. 100 p.

14. Lifelong education. *Educational documentation and information* (Geneva, IBE), 46th year, no. 185, 4th quarter 1972, 61 p.

15. Phillips, H.M. *Planning educational assistance for the Second Development Decade.* Paris, Unesco: International Institute for Educational Planning, 1973. 75 p. (Fundamentals of educational planning, 18.)

16. Thomas, A.N.; Diamond, Naomi. *Changes in secondary education and their implications for continuing education in Canada.* Paris, Unesco: IBE, 1973. 26 p. (Experiments and innovations in education, no. 5.)

17. *Prospects: quarterly review of education* (Paris, Unesco). See particularly: vol. 2, no. 3, autumn 1972, on adult education; vol. 3, no. 3, autumn 1973, on secondary education, training and employment; vol. 3, no. 4, winter 1973, on the European university in change; vol. 4, no. 2, summer 1974, on international aid for educational development.

C. Publications by other international organizations

18. Council of Europe. Council for Cultural Co-operation. *Permanent education: a compendium of studies.* Strasbourg, 1970. 509 p.

19. Organization for Economic Co-operation and Development. International movement of scientists and engineers. Paris, 1970.

20. ——. New relations between post-secondary education and employment. Paris, 1973. (ED/73/13.)

21. ——. Quantitative trends in post-secondary education (1960-1970). Paris, 1973. (ED/73/7.)

22. ——. *Short-cycle higher education: a search for identity.* Paris, 1973. 414 p.

23. ——. Centre for Educational Research and Innovation. *The management of innovation in education.* Paris, 1972. 67 p.

24. Schaeffknecht, J.J. *Le métier de formateur.* Strasbourg, Council of Europe, 1971.

D. Other works

25. Caceres, B. *Regards neufs sur les autodidactes.* Paris, Editions du Seuil, 1961. 207 p.

26. Coombs, P.H.; Posser, R.C.; Manzoor, A. *New paths to learning for rural children and youth.* New York, International Council for Educational Development, 1973. 133 p., bibl.

27. Coombs, P.H.; Manzoor, A. *Attacking rural poverty: how non-formal education can help.* A research report for the World Bank, edited by Barbara Baird Israel. Baltimore, Johns Hopkins University Press, 1974. 292 p., fig., bibl.

28. Eurich, A.C. *Reforming American education.* New York, Harper & Row, 1969. 269 p., bibl.

29. Freire, P. *Pédagogie des opprimés,* suivi de *Conscientisation et révolution.* Paris, Maspero, 1974. 202 p., bibl.

30. ——. *L'éducation: pratique de la liberté.* Paris, Cerf, 1971. 154 p., fig.

31. Freeman, J. *Team teaching in Britain.* London, Ward Lock International, 1969. 424 p., fig., bibl.

32. Goulet, R.R., ed. *Educational change: the reality and the promise.* New York, Citation Press, 1968. 286 p.

33. Gourévitch, J.P. *Défi à l'éducation.* Paris, Casterman, 1973. 202 p., fig., bibl.

34. Hassenforder, J. *L'innovation dans l'enseignement.* Paris, Casterman, 1972. 144 p., bibl.

35. Havelock, R.G. *A guide to innovation in education.* Ann Arbor, Mich., University of Michigan, 1970. Various pagings, bibl.

36. Heiss, A. *An inventory of academic innovation and reform.* Berkeley, Calif., The Carnegie Commission on Higher Education, 1973. 123 p.

37. Husén, T.; Boalt, G. *Educational research and educational change: the case of Sweden.* New York, Wiley, 1967. 233 p., fig.

38. Huteau, M.; Lautrey, J. *L'éducation à Cuba.* Paris, Maspero, 1967. 250 p., fig.

39. Illich, I. *Une société sans école.* Paris, Seuil, 1971. 189 p.

40. Lorenzetto, Anna. The cultural dimension of adult education. *Convergence* (Toronto), vol. VI, nos. 3-4, 1973, p. 67-77.

41. Orring, J. *L'école en Suède: un aperçu sur l'enseignement primaire et secondaire.* Stockholm, SÖ-förlaget/Skolöverstyrelsen, 1968. 166 p., fig.

42. Piaget, J. *Où va l'éducation ?* Paris, Denoël/Gonthier, 1972. 138 p.

43. Rathborne, C.H. *Open education: the informal classroom.* New York, Citation Press, 1971. 207 p., fig.

44. Rogers, E.M.; Shoemaker, F.F. *Communication of innovation: a cross-cultural approach.* 2nd ed. New York, Free Press, 1971. 476 p., fig., bibl.

45. Saedeleer, H. de. *De Open Universiteit: projecten en realisaties in vijf landen.* Gent, Centrum voor vergelijkende studies vor het hoger onderwijs, 1973. 81 p., fig. [Abstract in English]

46. Silberman, C.E. *Crisis in the classroom.* New York, Random House, 1970. 553 p.

47. Vaizey, J. *The political economy of education.* London, Duckworth, 1972. 227 p., fig.

48. Young, M. *Innovation and research in education.* London, Routledge & Kegan Paul, 1965. 184 p.

Index